THE FORTEAN TIMES BOOK OF

CLOSE SHAVES
AND AMAZING LUCK

THE FORTEAN TIMES BOOK OF

CLOSE SHAVES
AND AMAZING LUCK

COMPILED BY STEVE MOORE

ILLUSTRATIONS BY ED TRAQUINO

JOHN BROWN PUBLISHING

First published in Great Britain in August 1999
by John Brown Publishing Ltd, The New Boathouse,
Bramley Road, London W10 6SR, UK.
Tel 0171 565 3000. Fax 0171 565 3050.

First impression August 1999

ISBN 1 902212 185

Printed and bound in Great Britain by
Creative Print and Design (Wales) Ebbw Vale, Gwent

CONTENTS

Lady Luck — we've all appealed to her for aid at some time or other. Rather fewer of us may actually have cause to thank her for it and, on occasion, it has to be said that she helps out in a pretty back-handed fashion. After all, you may be lucky to be alive if you've just had a six-foot steel crowbar driven through one side of your skull and out the other, but most of us would rather we didn't actually need that sort of luck in the first place. Maybe she just has a peculiar sense of humour.

A few years back we produced *Life's Losers*, a book of bad luck stories (and some of them were very bad luck stories), but this time we flip the coin and come up with life's winners ... or at least the folks who've won through with their lives. Waking up in the mortuary, plummeting miles without a parachute, falling into a mincing machine and coming out almost intact, cutting one's own throat with a chainsaw and living to croak the tale... or being rescued at sea by a man on a giant inflatable lobster. But just in case you think Lady Luck's only expression is a rather lop-sided (and occasionally malevolent) grin, we've thrown in a few tales where she has the sweetest of smiles, reuniting lost families, returning personal treasures or giving her favourites the winning touch. But maybe that's just a mask...

Many of the stories collected here are cream-of-the-crop offerings which have already appeared in the pages of *Fortean Times*, supplemented by a whole bunch more from our over-flowing archives which didn't make it into print for lack of space. We have to make the usual disclaimer, of course... we can't say with absolute certainty that every story presented here is one hundred per cent true, but they have all appeared in the press at some time or other (and yes, we've tried to avoid some of the tabloids at the ropier end of the market!). Maybe some of these folks just couldn't get that lucky... but we don't have the time, or the luck, to be able to check on every tale. We can provide our source references for each story, and these will be found in a separate section at the end of the book. Whether you want to believe everything you read in the papers, though, is up to you!

As always, enormous thanks are due to the legion of clipsters world-wide who continue to feed *Fortean Times* with news stories from all four corners of the globe (so to speak). We're lucky to have such enthusiastic support, and it's much appreciated. And thanks, of course, to our readers, one and all. May you never be too closely-shaven... and may Lady Luck smile (not too weirdly) on you all!

Steve Moore

UP IN THE AIR

High in the sky and closer to heaven... maybe divine
intervention has something to do with these ærial escapes.

A WING AND A PRAYER got Air-Inter flight 903 from Orly
airport in Paris to Lourdes in October 1993. The plane was
carrying a multi-faith mission to the shrine for a conference on
miracles, but got off to a bad start with one runway being occu-
pied by striking Air France ground staff. Despite 40 years'
experience, the pilot made several astonishing errors once in
the air, prompting the assembled priests, mullahs, and rabbis
to intercede loudly and urgently for divine assistance. At 5,000
feet the plane suddenly fell out of the sky. When the plummeting began and the cabin lights failed, the passengers were
simply told they had hit air turbulence.

In fact, neither pilot nor co-pilot had remembered to with-
draw the undercarriage, and on noticing the noise of air resis-
tance they shut down the engines by mistake. After restarting
them, the pilot then switched them off again in error, and the
plane disappeared from Orly's radar. Somehow the engines

were restarted again at 1,500 feet, and the plane landed safely at Lourdes. Perhaps all that praying had something to do with it. The pilot was promptly marched off to face an enquiry.

FARMER ELDON FERGUSON, 44, was flying with friends in a hired Cessna from Quebec to Newfoundland in late 1997 when a mystery explosion blew away the front of the aircraft. He fell 5,000 feet, but landed unhurt in a snow drift. The plane's other occupants were less fortunate and didn't survive.

PERHAPS EVEN LUCKIER was nine-year-old Erika Delgado, the sole survivor from a DC-9 which blew up in mid-air in 1995, 10 miles from the Colombian city of Cartagena, the wreckage falling 14,000 feet into a swamp. All 52 passengers and crew were killed except Erika, who was thrown out of the burning plane by her mother, and landed on a thick cushion of water lilies. She had broken arms, a broken leg, an abdominal injury, and her gold necklace was stolen by a pair of looters before a group of farmers found her and took her to a neighbouring village. But she survived, and was discharged from hospital 11 days later.

IT SHOULD have only been an hour's flight across Kansas, when Dr Bob Frayser set off in December 1997 from his hometown of Hoisington for Topeka. But the Piper Comanche 400 had a crack in the engine exhaust which allowed carbon monoxide to seep into the cabin's heating system, and 30 minutes into the flight Dr Frayser, alone at the controls, passed out. Fortunately, he'd set the auto-pilot soon after leaving Grand Bend airport, and the plane continued on course at a steady 5,500 feet... for about two hours, until it ran out of fuel over Missouri, with Frayser still unconscious at the controls. Then it landed itself, skidding 500 feet on its belly before crashing into trees in a meadow near the town of Cairo. Frayser awoke disoriented, with a ringing in his ears and a terrible headache. He had a broken wrist, a few cuts above his left eye, and bruised ribs from the seat-belt. "Most credit I give to the Lord," he said.

LESS RESPONSIBLE, but perhaps even more lucky, was the six-man crew of a Soviet military transport who lost control of the aircraft in mid-air after a heavy drinking session. The incident apparently happened in 1989, and was prompted by an unscheduled three-day stopover at a Russian airbase. The crew progressively drunk themselves into a stupor as they waited for the weather to clear, and then took off without securing a cabin door. As the oxygen level in the plane dropped, all six blacked out while the aircraft lurched aimlessly through the air for more than an hour... with the automatic pilot switched off. When the co-pilot woke up, a little more sober than he was before, he radioed: "Where are we? Where are we flying? I feel terrible!" Apparently none the wiser, he managed to land the plane in a snowfield.

ACCORDING TO MEDICAL LORE, it's supposed to be impossible to survive a flight at 36,000 feet while stowing away in the undercarriage of an aircraft, but that's what 13-year-old Guillermo Rosales did in 1993. If he hadn't been crushed by the wheel coming up, lack of oxygen and temperatures between 28 to 34 degrees below zero centigrade should have done for him. Fortunately, though, the wheel-well was pressurised, and he tumbled out of the DC-8 in Miami, after a three-hour flight from Colombia, "looking like a ball of snow". A short visit to hospital set him right, and he was even more lucky in that he wasn't repatriated. He had been living out of garbage cans at Bogota airport before hitching the ride.

CHAPTER ONE

INCREDIBLE AS IT SOUNDS, the pilot of a light aircraft and his passenger claim to have escaped unhurt after stuffing their cargo of soft cheese into the cockpit to absorb the impact when their plane crash-landed in Wisconsin in 1995. Passenger Frank Emmert, 36, said: "We were smelly but alive."

A PILOT in Austria was flying solo at 3,000 feet in a Cessna in 1992, when he saw a car somersault off a lonely road and land in a field. With no help in sight, he radioed for an ambulance and flew on. When he landed half an hour later, he learned that his prompt action had helped save the lives of the car's occupants... his own wife and children.

A WOBBLY BOEING 707 cargo jet took off from Miami airport in July 1997, but rapidly slipped from 1,000 feet to less than a hundred, and then hurtled along Biscayne Boulevard in downtown Miami, trailing black smoke. The pilot told air traffic control that he was having problems with the yaw damper, which prevents wobbling from side to side. Occupants of the First Union building actually looked down on the plane as it flew past with its wings flapping up and down, and it then narrowly missed the big electric guitar sign on the Hard Rock Café, navigated between the twin six-storey Royal Caribbean International buildings and vanished out of sight. The yaw damper problem had somehow corrected itself, and the plane continued north to New York and Gander, Newfoundland.

DES MALONEY, 28, suffered from premature ejection in April 1994 when he was catapulted from the cockpit of a Provost jet piloted by his elder brother, Tom, as it flew upside down at 250 mph. The ejector seat fired accidentally at 3,000 feet, hurling him through the plastic canopy and then sending him spinning to earth with a parachute that not only failed to open properly, but began to strangle him as well. He landed in a field outside a supermarket near Colchester, but suffered no serious injuries, spending only one day in hospital, while his brother managed to control the plane and land safely, 20 miles away. The first person on the scene when Des landed was a 14-year-old boy, who asked him for his parachute.

A GOOD AND BAD LUCK story from Northampton, Connecticut: Alfred Peters, 51, a former army paratrooper, jumped from a plane at 8,000 feet in November 1993, in a zone that was supposed to be reserved for sky-divers. Seconds later, as he fell at about 100 mph, he suddenly saw a Piper Cherokee flying toward him and, though he dipped his shoulder in an attempt to avoid it, the next thing he knew there was a thud. Peters had struck the upright fin of the plane's tail so hard that it broke. He still managed to pull the rip-cord, and landed safely with no more than a broken ankle. The plane, unfortunately, was so badly damaged that it went into a spin and crashed, killing all four aboard.

It might be thought that Peters' escape was unique, but no – in October 1996, pretty much the same thing happened again over Belval in north-east France, with far happier consequences. Sky-diver Martal Troyon, 40, jumped from a plane at 15,000 feet, and 5,000 feet below he landed on the wing of a glider from Luxembourg, piloted by Jean-Marc Slana. He saw the glider five seconds before he hit it, but his evasive action failed, and all he could do was lay flat to try to lessen the impact. Striking at 120 mph, he cracked the fibre-glass wing and then, winded and bruised, clung on for a short time while the two men stared at each other. Then Troyon let go of the wing, cleared the plane and opened his parachute. Both men landed okay, shocked but unharmed. Who paid for the damaged wing isn't recorded.

HANG-GLIDER PILOT Steve Clark, 32, escaped death twice in April 1993, when he crashed into power lines at Brentwood, Essex. The lines were carrying 275,000 volts, and his metal-frame glider bounced off one line and hit another; but he escaped electrocution because he didn't touch both lines at the same time. After that, he plunged 150 feet to the ground, surrounded by a shower of sparks and, though he was taken to hospital with head and leg injuries, he survived again.

AN ÆROFLOT JET carrying 55 passengers landed safely in Arkhangelsk, Russia, in May 1994, despite a loss of hydraulic fluid that prevented the full use of its landing gear. The crew solved the problem by pouring all the lemonade on board into the hydraulic system.

A similar, if rather more embarrassing problem struck Steve and Kathy Swigard as the flew their Cessna near Lake Tahoe, California, about the same time but they had no lemonade on board. Instead they urinated into the hydraulic system, creating just enough pressure to get the landing gear down.

ON STEWART ISLAND, New Zealand, Maurie Treweek was sitting on the tail of a Cessna 172 in April 1992, as it taxied for position on a beach, in winds of 20 knots. He was using his weight to keep the light aircraft's tail down, but it worked rather too well – the nose came up, the plane took off with Treweek still aboard, and started to swing out to sea. As his body was jammed against the rudder, though, the plane circled and started back toward the beach, at which point he started inching along the fuselage, changing his weight-position in a bid to help pilot Brian Grant control the aircraft. All to no avail – the plane dipped and a wing hit the water, flinging him off. Neither he nor Grant were injured, but the plane was wrecked. "I have got a big god who's looking after me," Treweek said.

IT SHOULD HAVE BEEN a routine holiday flight from Birmingham to Malaga, but things went seriously wrong for British Airways flight 5390 shortly after take-off in June 1990. All six windows on the cockpit of the BAC 111 had been replaced less than a week before, but one of them suddenly blew out, 23,000 feet over Oxfordshire. Captain Timothy Lancaster, 40, was sucked out of his seat, sliding under his locked safety belt and, despite grabbing on to the controls, was pulled through the three-foot gap in front of him onto the plane's nose-cone. Fortunately, two stewards were in the cockpit at the time, and one of them managed to grab the Captain's legs, holding onto him until the other steward managed to strap himself into the pilot's seat and get hold of him instead. But they couldn't pull Lancaster back into the cockpit.

With 81 shocked passengers aboard, the plane decompressing, and the air temperature at minus 20 degrees centigrade, an oxygen mask was placed on co-pilot Alistair Atcheson's face, and he brought the plane down for an emergency landing at Southampton, 15 minutes later – with Lancaster still dangling through the window. Blood and pieces of shirt were smeared over the aircraft fuselage, but Lancaster escaped with frostbite and fractures to his elbow, wrist and thumb. More importantly, all the passengers and crew escaped with their lives.

A PET DOG saved Ravi Bhatiasevi's life... by biting him. He was in so much pain that he cancelled his flight booking from Bangkok to Kathmandu, in September 1992. The plane crashed en route, killing all 113 people on board.

THE PILOT of a Delta Airline Boeing 737 looked out of his cockpit window as he flew between Pittsburgh and Atlanta in June 1987, and suddenly saw a four-foot missile-like object

CHAPTER ONE

heading toward his plane. It eventually passed to one side and slightly below the plane, which was flying at 29,500 feet. Investigations by the Federal Aviation Authority failed to establish where the missile came from or where it went, and both the Weather Service and the military denied responsibility. All we have is a near-miss from a near-missile... and no end to the story.

BITING THE BULLET

When the bullet has your name on it, there's no getting out of the way. But that doesn't mean you're dead...

TWO MEN burst into a post office in Battersea, London, in 1993, and opened fire. A 9mm bullet went through the armoured glass screen and hit postmistress Bharti Patel, only two feet away, in the mouth. It ricocheted off her teeth and span out through her cheek. Though injured, she survived the attack.

ANOTHER ORAL ESCAPE for nightclub boss John Monzouros, 30, who was shot in the mouth by a crazed drinker in London's Ferdenzis Club in March 1992. The bullet passed in and out of his jaw, neck, shoulder and back without hitting any vital organs.

ONLY THREE DAYS into a year-long mission to the Philippines, Dr Andrew Douglas-Dixon, a 38-year-old medical doctor and Mormon missionary from Yorkshire, found himself in the midst of an armed robbery in a Manila chemist shop called Bong Lucky. The gang opened fire indiscriminately, killing the man beside him, and a shop assistant was seriously injured by flying glass. Shortly afterwards, five others, including two policemen, died in a battle with the gunmen. Douglas-Dixon was himself hit by five bullets, two in the right hand, one in the left foot, and one in the right foot, where the bullet was stopped by the heel of his boot. The fifth bullet would probably have been fatal, but it hit squarely in his back-pack, passed through four books and came to rest in a hardback Filipino translation of the *Book of Mormon*. That bullet threw him forward against the counter, breaking his arm and a few fingers. He was flown home to Bradford for treatment, but intended to return to Manila when his wounds were healed.

FALSE TEETH came to the rescue of cab driver Ignatius Nwandilibe, 47, in June 1992. He was shot in the mouth by a teenaged robber in Denver, Colorado. The bullet cut his lip and tongue, shattered his dentures, which slowed its speed and probably saved his life, before bullet fragments lodged in the roof of his mouth. The attacker fled, but that wasn't the end of Nwandilibe's problems: the police held his shattered teeth as evidence. Such dental escapes are not as rare as might be thought. *Fortean Times* has at least four other similar cases on file.

IT LOOKED LIKE DIVINE INTERVENTION when a gunman opened fire at Helen Chavez's car in Los Angeles in 1998. The bullet deflected off a tiny statuette of Christ on the dashboard, and missed her completely.

TWO TALES of detouring bullets: in January 1975, Teresa Haro was working in a shop in Los Angeles when a gunman fired a shot into her face from close range. The bullet hit Mrs Haro above the nose, bounced off her skull, skidded under her skin and emerged above her forehead. Detective Joe Beiro said he'd never seen anything like it, but only a few months before Frankie Lane, a British soldier serving in Belfast, was hit by a sniper's bullet. It went up his nose, round his skull, and came out of his ear.

PATROLMAN TED CARLTON was chasing two escaped convicts in Oklahoma City in 1975 when a bullet smashed through his car windscreen. That reduced the bullet's energy just enough that it was finally stopped by the thin metal frames of his spectacles, and his only injury was a gashed cheek.

SOMETIMES, MONEY BUYS YOU LUCK. Hiroshi Oyama, a 62-year-old dentist from Osaka, Japan, was confronted by a middle-aged, mustachioed gunman outside his house after returning from a late dinner in January 1992. "Are you Mr Oyama?" he asked. As soon as Oyama replied "Yes", the man fired once into his chest, jumped into a car and drove off. Oyama, who had no idea why he was shot at, was uninjured. The bullet was found lodged halfway through a bundle of 42 banknotes, amounting to 242,000 yen (£1,084), in his fold-over wallet. So much for credit cards being a safer way to carry your money...

HAVING ENOUGH CREDIT CARDS may do the trick, however. When a mugger in North Brunswick, New Jersey, blasted 62-year-old Herb Kravitz in the chest in April 1993, the bullet ricocheted off his card-crammed wallet. He escaped without even a bruise.

RETIRED POLICEMAN Charles Kobel, 50, of New York City, was confronted by a mugger in 1991, who demanded his watch and wallet. He was complying when the mugger pronounced the fatal words "I might as well kill you anyway," aimed at Kobel's neck and fired. The .22 calibre bullet was deflected by the knot in Kobel's tie, after which he drew his own gun and the mugger fled. He was treated for powder burns to his neck.

RETURNING TO THEIR CAR after an evening at the ballet in March 1992, Dr John M Rainey and his wife Carol were confronted by a robber on the street in Cleveland, Ohio. The man pulled a gun and demanded money. Rainey tried to push the gun away, but the man brought it back toward him and fired, then ran off. The doctor didn't realise he was wounded until he was in the police station reporting the incident. Police examining his overcoat noticed blood and a bullet tear, and as a bloody chequebook was removed from his breast pocket, a small-calibre bullet fell to the floor. It had gone right through the chequebook and broken his skin, but he was not seriously injured.

STRUCK BY THIRST, Ronnie Ware, 15, of Memphis, Tennessee, went to the kitchen sink for a glass of water in 1990. Suddenly a bullet zipped through the window's two panes of glass and a heavy curtain, straight into his open mouth. It struck a back tooth, chipped it, and dropped out of his mouth when he fell, knocked unconscious by the impact. He wasn't able to walk for two or three hours afterwards. Police arrested a suspect with a pellet gun, which can fire bullets up to .22 calibre with compressed air.

SECURITY EXPRESS was delivering £25,000 to the Midland bank in Poole, Dorset, in May 1987, and one of the guards was Albert Howard, 58. He was attacked by Londoner Stephen Kelt, 31, disguised in a wig and overalls, who thrust a revolver into his mouth and ordered him to hand over the money. Howard knocked the gun aside and got Kelt into a headlock. Kelt's accomplice, James Watts, smashed his gun into Howard's head and kicked him, but he wouldn't let go. Watts then fired at Howard's chest, Kelt struggled free, and the gang escaped with £2,000 in cash and some travellers' cheques. But Howard was saved by the power of prayer... Watts' .45 calibre bullet went through his diary and then ricocheted off the prayer book he always carried in his shirt pocket. There were powder burns on the shirt, but apart from bruises, Howard was unharmed. His attackers were later arrested on robbery and firearms charges.

A SUSPECTED DRUG DEALER fired at the chest of agent Carlos Montalvo of the Bureau of Alcohol, Tobacco and Firearms in Westland Shopping Mall, Hialeah, Florida, in 1987. But, incredibly, the bullet was stopped by Montalvo's own gun, lodging in the empty barrel. The agent was treated for facial cuts inflicted by fragments from his 9mm Sig Sauer pistol.

MALE READERS may want to skip this story. Angel Santana, 51, was shot with a .357 calibre Magnum pistol in January 1990, during a struggle with one of three men holding up the New York store where he worked. The bullet lodged in his trouser zipper and, according to police spokesman Fred Weiner, the robbers were so shocked that they fled, dropping the gun. He added that although the story seemed hard to believe, it had been double-checked by officers and the gun and spent bullet had been found in the store. Santana, unsurprisingly, was treated for trauma in hospital.

RANDOMLY FIRING YOUTHS on a piece of waste ground 125 yards away sent a .45 calibre bullet through the kitchen window of Ava Donner, of Pittsburgh, California, in 1993. She was unharmed, as the bullet struck a stainless steel spoon she was holding at the time. An inch either way, and it would have hit her in the chest.

AN UNNAMED ULSTER LOYALIST was shot by an undercover soldier in Belfast in March 1993. He cheated death when the bullet shattered a brass Chubb door key in his jacket pocket, deflecting it away from his body.

MOBILE PHONES may seem a curse to some folks, but to others they're real life-savers. Austria's top hostage negotiator, Colonel Friedrich Maringer, was dealing with a robber in June 1993, who'd holed up with hostages in a clothes shop after a botched bank-raid. Maringer had just negotiated the release of two hostages when the robber, who'd already killed one policeman, panicked and opened fire. The bullet was stopped by Maringer's mobile phone. It would otherwise have hit him in the heart, but he escaped with bruising.

SOME OF OUR TALES, it has to be said, do seem a mite inflated. But, according to our source, Dora Oberling, a 30-year-old stripper from Tampa, Florida, cheated death in October 1993 when a bullet fired at her by her 75-year-old lover was stopped by the silicone implant in her left breast. "Now all I need is a simple repair job and I'll be as good as new," she said. "I've also learned to stick with guys my own age in future."

SOMETIMES, we get a clue as to how these things work. An assassin's bullet missed the head of the Thai minister for science and technology, the unpronouncably named Mr Phisan Moonlasartsathorn, by a centimetre in April 1993. The minister, who's also an adviser to the Buddhist Image Club of Thailand, obviously has his own views on science and technology. He explained that the 'magnetic field' of a small Buddha amulet he wears 'deflected the bullet'. The amulet was given to him several years previously, after it had been taken from the body of a dead Cambodian soldier (who presumably hadn't been so lucky), and had apparently also saved him from a hail of gunfire in an earlier incident. He added that the amulet had 'invisible power' by virtue of 'natural science'. Natural?? Science??

RABBIT CATCHER Tony Southwell, 32, of Bassett, Southampton, was chasing vermin on a Winchester golf course in October 1993, when he spotted a man in combat gear running into a copse. The next thing he knew a shot rang out and he felt a bullet striking his waist. Fearing the worst, he looked down... and saw the shot had lodged in a rabbit hanging from his belt.

YOU WIN SOME, you lose some. Patrick Gayle, 33, was on his way to exchange $40-worth of losing lottery tickets for new ones when he paused to watch a teenage gunfight in Harrisburg, Pennsylvania, in April 1997. He got caught in the crossfire, and a bullet smashed through a lighter and credit cards before burying itself in the tickets. Gayle was unhurt. He passed his tattered wad of tickets to the police as evidence, then went on to play the lucky numbers again.

A WEEK LATER, it was a seller rather than a player who got lucky. Brazilian lottery ticket vendor Raimundo Dias Carneiro, from Belo Horizonte in Minas Gerais, escaped death when a gunman tried to rob his store. Four small coins in his breast pocket stopped the bullet. "These coins are blessed", he remarked.

A COIN was involved in our next story too, but this time things worked out slightly differently. In October 1982, an attempted murder by a shotgun raider at the Glebe pub in Stechford,

Birmingham, was foiled when landlord Brendan Dempsey bent down to pick up a penny from the pub-floor. Unaware of the danger, he ducked just as the gun went off, and the shot went harmlessly over him. The raider fled.

IT'S NOT ALWAYS bullets involved in these stories, of course. A boy of 14 from Middlesbrough survived a stabbing attack in February 1997, when he was mugged in an underpass. The mugger stabbed him in the chest, but the blade was stopped by a tin of mints in his breast pocket.

MAYBE IT WAS FORESIGHT, but Terry Shafer decided to give her policeman husband David his Christmas present early in December 1977. It was a bulletproof vest and, yes, the first evening he wore it, a thief fired a pistol straight at his stomach. He escaped with a painful bruise. Even more surprisingly, it was said to be the first ever armed robbery in Bettendorf, Iowa.

IT BEGAN as an ordinary traffic dispute about not being allowed to overtake, when James Janecke, 25, and his girlfriend were driving in Chandler, Arizona, in December 1992. Eventually, though, Leonard Peralta drew a gun and shot Janecke in the head, just above the right temple. Janecke was taken to hospital in Mesa, still conscious, and his nose began to bleed in the emergency room. A police officer handed him a towel, he blew his nose... and blew out the .22 calibre bullet, which had apparently been lodged in his sinus cavity. Janecke was released after treatment, and Peralta was arrested for aggravated assault with a deadly weapon.

ANOTHER TRAFFIC DISPUTE led to a shoot-out between rival gangs in Torrance, California, in May 1993. Rafaela Ramos, 33, was standing a short distance away, with friends, when she caught a stray bullet. Her life was saved when the .22 calibre slug embedded itself in her wide, choker-type, gold necklace.

ANYONE WHO THINKS that comic-strip cat Garfield is a ghastly little beast will be heartened by the following tale. Cynthia Guerrero, 5, was riding in the family pick-up truck in Corpus Christi, Texas, in September 1989, when someone took a shot at the vehicle. Cynthia escaped with facial cuts when the .22 calibre bullet shattered the window, but the shot was deflected by a stuffed Garfield toy, attached to the glass with suction cups. Police said they didn't know who fired the shot, or why. Maybe the gunman just wanted to let the cat have it...

CHILEAN PRESIDENT Augusto Pinochet survived an assassination attempt in 1986, when gunmen opened fire on his motorcade. Maybe it was just luck, but Pinochet noticed that the assassins' bullets had formed the image of the Virgin Mary on the armour-plating of his blue Mercedes, and became convinced that his life had been spared by divine intervention.

AND NOW, the one you've been waiting for: "bullet deflected by ham sandwich"! A teenager walked into Jose Fana's grocery store in New York in March 1994 and ordered a ham and cheese sandwich. Fana, 39, wrapped the sandwich in paper and was about to hand it over when the teenager pulled out a gun and fired. Fana shielded his head with the sandwich, and escaped with only a grazing wound.

GOOD LUCK doesn't always last. Hector Cuevas, 33, was a Chilean police officer who became a national celebrity in November 1995 when a bank robber's bullet was stopped by a pen inside his pocket, and he suffered only an ink stain. In June 1996, a eucalyptus tree fell on his squad car and crushed him.

IT WAS JUST THERE...

It isn't just escapes we have to thank Lady Luck for ...
sometimes she hands out gifts, too.

FOR THE SECOND TIME in five days, a man out searching for bamboo shoots found a bag containing 100m yen (approximately £434,000) in the same thicket near Tokyo, in 1989. The money was eventually traced to one Kazuyasu Noguchi, a company president who had made a fortune dealing in stamps. His story sounds unlikely, to say the least: he said that, rather than pay tax, he had left the money in the bamboo hoping that whoever picked it up would donate it to charity.

ALSO IN JAPAN, and also in 1989, there was more luck for a garbage collector demolishing a safe at a rubbish dump in Yokohama. This turned out to contain the equivalent of £757,575 which belonged to Haruo Nakanishi, formerly a senior executive of the Buddhist movement Soka Gakkai. Nakanishi, had apparently simply left the safe in the warehouse of a newspaper he published and forgotten about it. Police remained sceptical about this tale, especially when it turned out that the money was actually the takings from a souvenir shop near the movement's main temple, which had not been declared for tax.

THE FIRST piece of good luck for Liliana Parodi was that she didn't have to pay for her pasta in her favourite restaurant in Genoa, Italy, in April 1996, after finding it contained a small stone which wedged in her teeth. The second was that, when the stone was removed the next day, it turned out to be an uncut diamond worth almost £2,000.

IT SOUNDED LIKE A FAIRYTALE, but Zbigniew Leszczynski wrote to the *Guardian* newspaper in 1989, claiming it was true. He had been fishing in the River Coquet in Northumberland when he saw a rainbow spring from a particular spot on the river bank. This was followed by heavy rain and a flood, but two days later he passed the same place where the rainbow had touched the ground. Floodwater swirled round a little hillock of sand and gravel, 18 inches high, and on the top of it was a gold signet ring. He took it to the local police station, where no one claimed it, and a few months later it was given to its lucky finder. So it seems you can find gold at the end of the rainbow...

CHILDREN CHASING A SCORPION through the ruins of a mediæval fort in Yeola, western India, in 1994, found a pitcher stuffed full of silver coins from the era of the Mogul empire. The coins were of various dates between 1556 and 1707.

IN BOCHUM, Germany, five-year-old Nicole Ohlsen found a doll on a rubbish-tip in 1996, and took it home. Her mother

Ute was about to throw it out when she discovered £45,000 worth of diamonds hidden inside. After checks failed to turn up an owner, police told the family they could keep the gems, which were to be used to pay for Nicole's education.

THREE ORPHANS in Sierra Leone, whose parents had been killed two years previously during a rebel attack on their village of Hinnah Malen, went searching for wild yams in January 1997, after two days without food. Morie Jah, 14, the eldest of the boys, said they were returning home after a fruitless three hour search when they found a yam under a palm tree. Underneath it was a flawless 100-carat diamond, which valuers in the capital, Freetown, said was worth at least £325,000.

A NUMBER of residents in Tucson, Arizona, were puzzled in January 1999 when they found $100 bills in their mailboxes. Some had as many as three. Others, of course, may not have said how many they found. Police had no idea who left the money or why.

IT WAS NO GREAT SUM, but when fishmonger Roger Woestyn opened up a small shark caught at Nieuport, off the coast of Belgium, he found an English £5 note inside, smelly but tenable. That was back in 1975, when a £5 note was still worth something; now it'd be more economical to save the fish and throw the money away.

HORRORS!

Not for the faint-hearted or weak-stomached,
this chapter. The luckiest thing to be said of these
survivors is... they lived!

FORTHMAN MURFF had a wonderful name and wonderful
luck too. The 74-year-old lumberjack was cutting timber near
his home in Gattman, Mississippi, in 1984, when a big branch
fell from a tree and knocked him backwards into a ditch, and
onto the still-whirring chainsaw he was holding. It sliced across
his neck, severing his windpipe, most of the neck muscles, two
external jugular veins and an internal one, leaving only his spine
and carotid artery intact. He threw the chainsaw off immediately, but as if that wasn't bad enough, another tree fell on him,
brought down by the branch, and broke his left leg and crushed
his foot. But the blood was only flowing in a stream, rather
than in spurts, so he thought he might still have a chance.
Digging himself out from under the tree, he managed to hobble to his truck and drive half a mile to a neighbour's house,
who loaded him into another truck and drove him to hospital

in nearby Amory. And, astonishingly, Murff lived to tell the tale. Sawdust sparked an infection in the wounds, and he had to be given a tracheotomy to help him breathe... but he believed that God had spared him to take care of his ailing wife. As if he didn't need taking care of himself!

ANOTHER ELDERLY VICTIM with similar luck was Arthur Cross, 70, a farmer living near St Louis, Missouri. Also in 1984, he was thrown from his tractor onto the vehicle's power-saw, and was sliced across his abdomen, from the left rib-cage, across his liver, bowels and genitals, before his son pulled him away. He was still conscious when a helicopter brought him to a hospital in St Louis, and underwent six days of surgery to put him back together again.

IN A DISPUTE over an inheritance in 1997, two relatives of 55-year-old Iranian Khadijeh Iran-Nejad threw her down an old well, then flung boulders down on top of her to make sure she was dead. The boulders missed her, and instead cracked a channel under the well's floor. She survived for 22 days by soaking a piece of cloth in water seeping from the cracks and sucking it, before eventually being rescued when a passerby heard her cries for help.

CONSTRUCTION WORKER Andrew Jepson, 26, survived being run over by a four-ton road-roller in January 1998. The roller was reversing at a noisy building site at Heathrow airport and caught Jepson's leg while his attention was diverted. He was unable to escape, and the machine rolled over his entire body while he lay face down. Rather than try to stop, the driver accelerated the roller to its maximum speed of 7 mph to ensure it was on top of Jepson for the minimum amount of time, and he was saved by his hard-hat and the uneven surface of pebble, shale and mud that was the foundation of a new road. He remained fully conscious throughout and escaped with cuts, bruising, crushed ribs and a collapsed left lung. Spending two days in intensive care, he was allowed home six days later.

SLEEPWALKER James Currens, 77, wandered off from his home in Palm Harbor, Florida, in November 1998. It probably seemed like a nightmare at first, but it was all real enough when he woke to find himself in a pool of water a few feet deep, with his legs stuck in mud, and several alligators, some over three feet long, closing in hungrily. Fortunately, his sleeping brain had remembered to take his walking stick along, and he managed to poke the beasts away while yelling for help. A neighbour heard his cries and called the police, who used lights to scare the alligators away before freeing Currens, who suffered only minor injuries.

THE LUCK OF THE IRISH held good for John Delaney, 56, in 1979. He was walking past a building site in Birmingham when a huge concrete coping stone, weighing at least a hundredweight, fell two floors and landed squarely on his unprotected head. Horrified police, ambulancemen and doctors expected him to die from massive brain damage, but the next day he sat up in his hospital bed and remarked: "I've got a bit of a headache, that's all." He also had a fractured skull and a cut requiring 17 stitches, but swiftly recovered.

YOUNG MOTHER Christina Stilts, 18, of Hampstead, Texas, abandoned her new-born baby girl in a ditch, wrapped up in a plastic dustbin bag. The 6lb 12oz baby was not found for 12 hours, and would have suffocated but for thousands of vicious fire ants which ate their way into the bag to get at her, thus letting air in through the holes. The baby was eventually found alive, covered from head to toe in ants, but was otherwise okay. Her mother faced up to 10 years in jail for abandoning her.

TEXAS CONSTRUCTION WORKER Brett Cruz, 22, somehow managed to fire a four-inch nail into his own heart with a nail-gun, in December 1993. "I think I've been shot," he remarked to co-workers, with classic clichéd understatement. With similarly classic overstatement, those same co-workers told the press later that they could "see the nail pulsating with his heartbeat." Cruz was taken to hospital in San Antonio, and lived to tell the tale.

JUST AS ALARMING is the tale of Kenneth Blount, 17, who was working with other carpenters on the frame of a house in Baton Rouge, Louisiana, in July 1979. A colleague working above him suddenly yelled, lost his footing, and dropped a pneumatic hammer which landed on Blount's head. The impact triggered the hammer, which punched a nail deep into his head, midway between the crown and his right ear. Blount thought at first that he'd simply been hit by the hammer, and reached up expecting to find a bump... instead there was the head of the nail in his skull, jammed in so tight it couldn't be pulled out. His workmates panicked, and Blount himself had to calm them down, before being taken to hospital. The nail was removed in a two-hour operation by surgeon James Poche, who was astounded at Blount's "dumb luck." There was little tissue damage and he recovered well – and vowed to wear a safety helmet in future.

JAKIE DALE KLABER probably didn't think he was lucky when the wind caught an 8 by 12 foot wooden concrete form panel that he was hoisting with a crane at a construction site in

Louisville, Kentucky, in November 1988. The panel blew into the wooden crane cab where Klaber, 50, was working, knocking him over the edge, and he plunged three floors before impaling himself on a 6-foot steel rod. It pierced his belly and groin, and there he hung until firefighters cut the rod and, with it still embedded in his body, lowered in a basket. He remained lucid enough to discuss his medical history, and the rod was later removed in hospital. So where does the luck come into this? Although Klaber had fallen three floors when he hit, the rod was actually six floors up; without that breaking his fall, the nine-floor plunge would probably have killed him.

MINER CHARLIE BETHELL was working underground at Whitwell Colliery, near Worksop, Notts, in April 1985, when a nine-foot wooden post was dislodged from a conveyor belt and pierced him completely through the chest. Luckily, the two-inch thick stake both passed by his lungs and missed his heart. He was given morphine shots and the post was cut short, before he was taken to hospital with the ends protruding from both his front and back. Surgeons were amazed to find that, apart from the holes, his only injuries were a few torn muscles, and just eight days later he walked out of hospital and went home.

ONE LAST IMPALEMENT is probably enough... this is, after all, supposed to be a book about good luck! When rescuers investigated a car that had smashed into a tree in Boston, Massachusetts, in May 1981, they found 39-year-old John Thompson inside, his head pierced through by a seven-foot steel crowbar, of the type used to shift granite blocks. It had been on the back seat and had flown forward on impact, penetrating the back of Thompson's skull and protruding three feet from just above his left eye. Paramedics supported the bar with sand-bags and cut it fore and aft with a grinder saw, keeping the metal cool with water to avoid cooking Thompson's brain. He was taken to Boston City Hospital, where neuro-surgeon Joseph Ordia cut his left scalp along the hair-parting, picked out the fragments of shattered skull, and lifted out the bar. The 40 lb crowbar had smashed its way through the mid-brain just above the brain stem, and it left Thompson with considerable damage, particularly difficulty in talking and right-side paralysis. But with the help of therapy teams, he was able to hobble out of hospital after three months and go home to convalesce. Perhaps the most astonishing thing is that he was alive in the first place.

SNACK FACTORY worker Mike Mordue, 41, almost ended up as a snack himself, when he fell into a huge food mincer at Consett, Co. Durham, in April 1994. No-one seems to know quite how he fell in, but the whirling steel blades almost sev-ered his left hand and he was, apparently, only an inch from being beheaded, when a safety device cut in and stopped the motor. Rescuers took 75 minutes to free him from the four-foot food vat, and he was taken to hospital where surgeons stitched back his hand.

ARGENTINE LABOURER Pedro Olivera walked home drunk after a brawl in February 1997 and fell asleep for four hours without realising he had a knife buried in his neck. Thirty-six -year-old Olivera, nicknamed "The Cat" for surviving three previous stabbings, only became aware of his wound when he looked in the mirror. His wife failed to extract the knife (perhaps fortunately), and called an ambulance. In hospital he told police he was unable to answer their questions, as he remembered nothing about the night of the brawl.

ON THE ROAD

Racing along the highway to hell...
and coming back alive!

KIM WON-SUN, 35, a Korean-born chef living in the USA, almost found himself cooked alive in a stunning serial-accident in May 1989. He was driving at around 60 mph on a highway near Washington when a tyre burst, sending him spinning out of control across four lanes of traffic, before smashing through railings on a bridge. The car then plunged 30 feet to land upside down on electrified railway tracks. Hanging upside down from his safety-belt, Kim remarked later that he felt as if he was "being spit-roasted," as the car roof sizzled and started to melt, with 750 volts going through it. At this point the car was rammed by an express train doing 70 mph and flung half a mile down the line. The door fell off, Kim scrambled clear... and trod on the live rail. But, a few seconds before, engineers had switched off the current and Kim emerged from his ordeal with nothing more than a four-inch gash on his elbow.

BAD LUCK FOR SOME is good for others. Two tractor-trailers loaded with paint supplies crashed in a fireball on Interstate 80 in Pennsylvania in August 1997, killing one driver. The resulting 12-hour traffic blockage left an awful lot of unhappy drivers, but also a clear strip of road. High above, John Storie was flying his family home to Houston, Texas, when their single-engined BE-35 started shaking and losing oil pressure. The cleared road made a perfect landing-strip, and Storie brought the plane down for a smooth landing.

CYCLING DOWN A STEEP HILL in Aalesund, Norway, nine-year-old Kristin Nalvik Loendal failed to stop at a junction and was hit by a car. Knocked off the bike, she went flying through the air, directly toward a truck full of vertically-stacked panes of glass going in the opposite direction. Miraculously, she somehow landed in the bed of the truck without hitting the glass, and escaped with a few bumps and bruises.

TWO CARS CRASHED and burst into flames on the M5 near Gloucester in June 1998... right in front of a van driven by fire-extinguisher salesman Phil Howard. He shouted to other motorists to take extinguishers from his van and, together, the impromptu fire service doused the flames.

THREE-YEAR-OLD Jennifer Simpson from Yeadon, West Yorkshire, swallowed a one pound coin in June 1998 and began coughing and struggling to breathe. Her parents, Alan and Linda Simpson, bundled her and her eight-year-old brother Thomas into the car and set off for the hospital in Otley, six miles away. Jennifer began to slip in and out of consciousness, and then the car skidded into the opposite lane on a hill, and was struck side-on by an oncoming van. The car was a write-off, though the only casualty was Thomas, who sustained a slight head wound. Meanwhile, the impact had dislodged the coin in Jennifer's throat, allowing her to breathe again. A passing motorist took Alan, Jennifer and Thomas to the hospital, where the coin was removed. If not for the accident, it was thought that she wouldn't have survived the remaining two minute journey to hospital.

THREE HOLIDAYMAKERS survived with little more than cuts and bruises when their Honda Civic collided head-on with a furniture delivery lorry near Newquay, Cornwall, in August 1998. This was no ordinary delivery lorry, though, because attached to its side was a 20 feet long by one foot wide metal girder, which became dislodged in the crash and shot forward, straight through the Honda. It entered through the windscreen, ripped off the driver's head-rest, tore through the back seats and finished up protruding 10 feet from the back of the car. Driver Stephen Gamory was missed by inches because the impact had thrown him forward into his airbag, though he suffered two cracked ribs. His nephew Andrew, 16, was asleep on the back seat, and was missed by a hair's breadth, while his brother Neil was unhurt in the front passenger seat.

ON A CAMPING TRIP to Ayers Rock, Cardiff taxi-driver Keith Evans crashed his truck in Western Australia's Great Victoria Desert, 200 miles from anywhere. As he lay there by the truck, battered and bruised, a rescuer appeared in the form of a wandering aborigine. However, unlike his forebears, renowned for their legendary skills in bush tracking and living off the land, this up-to-date saviour simply whipped out his mobile phone and called for help.

ALMOST IMITATING a TV advertisement where a Volvo car plunges from a building and lands intact and without harm to its crash-dummy occupant, an unnamed man in his 60s crashed his car backwards through a barrier on the fourth level of a multi-storey car-park in Canterbury, Kent, and plummeted 70 feet. The car landed upside down, caving in the roof and shattering the windows. Like the advert, the car was a Volvo and the driver survived... but, unlike the ad, he had to be pulled out of the car by firemen, and was taken to hospital with broken ribs and a head injury.

FORCED OUT of the army by a serious back injury, Angus Robb, 36, bought a Renault Laguna in August 1997, under the War Pensions Scheme. He had the vehicle modified and fitted with a swivel seat to help him get in and out. All was well until Mr Robb was driving along in Angus, Tayside, in September 1998, when he noticed a wisp of smoke by his right knee. He tried to pull over, but as he did so the central locking activated and flames started to lick up the side of the door, and the horn started blaring out. Mr Robb rang 999 on his mobile phone, then managed to crawl out through the jammed window, singeing his arm. By the time he got out, the car was well ablaze. A report later found the car to have no mechanical faults, so maybe it just had it in for him; but he escaped with no more than the most minor injuries.

ABSENT-MINDED FATHER Michael Murray of Millbury, Massachusetts, prepared to head home after visiting his wife at work, in 1995. He carefully strapped his 20-month-old daughter into her car-seat, but apparently completely forgot, because "the garage was dark", about three-month-old Matthew, whom he'd left sitting in another car-seat... on the car roof. After driving through busy city streets for some time, he pulled out onto Interstate Highway 290, accelerated, and then heard a scraping noise on the roof. At this point Murray looked around and realised that Matthew wasn't in the car, then looked in the mirror and saw his son sliding away down the highway. Fortunately, the driver behind, James Boothby, 67, managed to stop rather than swerve. He said: "I saw something in the air. I thought it was a doll. Then I saw the doll open its mouth. I couldn't believe it was a little baby." It was thought that Matthew's car-seat had helped him have a soft landing by creating a region of low air pressure above itself as it fell, like an aeroplane wing. The seat brand was "Guard With Glide".

KEVIN SLAUTER, a 32-year-old taxi-driver from Saltdean, East Sussex, was driving along the Brighton to Rottingdean road in April 1994 when he lost control of his car. It crashed through a safety fence and went over a cliff. However, because the car was a rear-engined Skoda, it fell tail-end first, and the back of the car and the engine absorbed most of the impact. Slauter survived the 150 foot fall with only minor fractures to his collar-bone, ribs and pelvis.

ALAN PRICE, 29, was sitting in his van at lunchtime in Bishopsgate, London, in October 1997, when high winds collapsed six floors' worth of metal scaffolding on a building close by. Tons of metal crashed down on the van and reduced it to a wreck no more than two feet high ... but somehow Price managed to crawl out completely unscathed. Perhaps just as miraculously, no one else was hurt in the accident either.

LUCKY ESCAPES from road accidents usually come singly, but in August 1994 the entire Preston family from Tynemouth was involved, when the Nissan Sunny they were travelling in plunged 50 feet onto a North Tyneside beach. The car was involved in a collision with another at the top of a cliff in Cullercoats, and was knocked across the road. It then crashed through iron safety rails, fell sideways down a 45-degree slope, hit a concrete wall, fell a further five feet onto a promenade, and came to rest on a wall with its rear in the air. As people began to run toward the car, its doors opened and the passengers got out. They were all completely unharmed, though the car was a write-off.

IT HELPS if you're in the right place at the right time, and 14-year-old Adrian Ball of Wrexham certainly was, in March 1974. Making his way along beside the road, a tanker-lorry suddenly overturned and crashed down right on the path where he was walking. But the cab crashed down in front of him, and the 20-ton load landed behind him, leaving Adrian in the space between. He was taken to hospital with a suspected broken arm, but driver Harry Bingham, who managed to get out of the cab unscathed, could only describe his escape as miraculous.

BRIAN KIRKHAM, 11, was in the right place too. He cheated death on his way to school in Bo'ness, West Lothian, in March 1995. As he was walking along, a lorry suddenly shed its load, and 24 tonnes of steel came hurtling toward him... only to stop at his feet. He escaped with a bruised toe.

MOVIE STUNTMEN do this sort of thing all the time, with careful preparation, but Richard Chapman, 38, found himself doing it for real, and without any time to think. Chapman was driving his Citroen BX near Lewes, East Sussex, in January 1993, when a 58-ton heavy goods lorry suddenly reversed out into the road in front of him. Unable to stop or swerve, he flattened himself across the front seats as the car hurtled under the lorry. The car roof was torn off and the seat-backs flattened – but when the car came to a halt, Chapman emerged unscathed.

A PLEASANT STROLL along cliffs at Santa Cruz, California, almost ended in disaster in March 1986. Pregnant Heidi Geoghegan and Richard Schraeder were walking near Lighthouse Point when a car, driven by a drunken teenage girl, went off the road, struck them, and plunged over the cliff. They went over the 20-foot cliff too, but Heidi landed on an abandoned couch on the rocks below. She and the baby were unharmed, and Richard was unhurt too; the girls in the car were taken to hospital with minor injuries... and were promptly arrested for drunken driving.

IT SOUNDS LIKE a movie car-chase: Bill Bees, 55, of Lockleaze, Bristol, was woken by the sound of screeching tyres outside one night in April 1992, and got up to see what was happening. Police were chasing a getaway car, and the robbers inside decided to divert the pursuit by throwing out the spare wheel... which then bounced off a curb and shot straight through Bill's first-floor bedroom window, crashing onto the bed where he'd been laying. There was said to be a skid-mark on the wall, and the room was wrecked, but Bees escaped unharmed.

FAT FRENCHMAN Jacques Mathely, 38, was saved by a spare tyre in May 1992 – his own! The 17-stone motorist was working under his Volvo saloon in Newbury, Berks, when the jack slipped and the car fell on him. But it bounced on his stomach and came to rest, saving him from having his head and chest crushed. He was eventually freed by firemen, and was duly thankful for his unhealthy lifestyle.

IT WAS TOO LATE to brake as Stuart Eaton headed straight for the smoke billowing from a car crash in front of him, on the Cirencester to Birdlip road in June 1992. With him in the

Peugeot was his girlfriend, Deborah Lander, and they just went straight through the smoke-cloud, emerging on the other side with no more than a broken headlamp and number plate having passed under the two colliding cars – a Metro and a Cavalier – as they span through the air overhead, toward opposite verges of the road.

A FRUIT SURPRISE for Tim Reeves, 44, his wife and teenage children, as they slept in their Suffolk cottage in January 1998. Good job they weren't in the living room, as during the night a lorry crashed and overturned in their garden, shedding its load – and an avalanche of apples thundered through the living room window. The driver was hurt, but the family awoke to find they had enough apples to keep the doctor away for many, many days...

MOBILE PHONES, love them or hate them, can sometimes be a blessing... even when they don't work. In July 1991, Tony Besant of Camberley, Surrey, was driving along the M3 at Basingstoke, Hants, when the car engine kept cutting out. He pulled over to the hard shoulder and tried to call the AA on his car phone, but that wasn't working either, so the 23-year-old driver abandoned his Ford Escort and set off in search of an emergency phone. Seconds after he'd left the car, he heard a screech, saw two giant trucks heading straight for him and the car, and took to his heels. The inevitable crash came, and when he looked back, one of the lorries had overturned on his car, flattening it. Besant was unharmed, but the motorway was blocked for two hours before the wreckage could be cleared.

SAVED BY THE...

Always expect the unexpected... and some of the rescuers
in these tales are very unexpected indeed.

LEAVING HIS VAN to open a gate in Cheddar, Somerset, 58-year-old Richard Stone forgot to apply the handbrake. The van moved forward and trapped him. His cries for help were heard 100 yards away by Sonny, a nine-year-old red-and-green macaw, who then began to mimic his cries. The squawks of "help!" alerted Richard Herd and Jeremy Burstow, who work at the park. They approached the bird, and then heard the human cries it was mimicking. The van was reversed off Mr Stone's leg and he escaped with severe bruising to his ankle.

IT'S NOT OFTEN that the gods intervene these days, but a shopkeeper in Hawaii decided to appease the Volcano goddess Pele by placing three leaves and a bottle of gin in the path of molten lava flowing from Mount Kilauea. After the lava had passed, all that was left of the village was a church and the prudent man's shop.

KRIS TAMER, an office manager at the Westland Convalescent Center in Detroit, misdialled a number in 1985 by transposing two digits, and hung up when she heard a gasping voice at the other end of the line. A colleague suggested she might have reached someone in need of help, so Tamer rang the number again. Alex Johnson, 81, was suffering from congestive heart failure, and just managed to give her his address. She rang the police, and helped to save his life.

THREE SEA SCOUTS took a dinghy out to sea in 1985, as part of a summer camp exercise at the mouth of the Blackwood River, near Augusta,Western Australia. In an attempt to retrieve a lost oar, their leader Vollert Asmussen, 41, his son Björn, and a friend, were swamped when the dinghy was hit by a wave. Strong currents swept them out into the Indian Ocean, and as they clung to the capsized dinghy, they became aware of a large whale nearby. It circled them for about an hour, then disappeared from view and surfaced underneath them. That lifted them up enough for Alan Wood, on the shore and looking for whales with a telescope, to spot the three men's heads bobbing up and down. He called a neighbour, and the Sea Scouts were rescued.

A YOUNG GIRL reclining on a set of blow-up teeth began to drift out to sea off the coast of Bexhill, East Sussex, in 1994, but was rescued by a man on a giant inflatable lobster. Two lifeboats were launched to save the girl, but the lobster reached her first. A coastguard spokesman remarked: "This sort of thing is all too common." Oh, really?

STUDENT DENISE BYRNE, 18, skidded off the road into a brook near Widnes, Cheshire, in November 1987. The car was sinking fast, but as the waters rose, Denise managed to clamber out onto the roof. And then suddenly she was rescued... by Batman! Tim Williamson, 20, was on his way home after a kissogram mission, still in full bat-regalia, and he sprang to the rescue and whisked her to safety. Denise was taken to hospital, safe but deeply shocked, though whether that resulted from the crash or from suddenly finding herself living in a comic-book is hard to tell.

SOME PEOPLE stay cool in a crisis, but it would be hard to beat Carl Diggle, 22, from Bolton. In August 1994, he actually stayed asleep when a fire broke out in his kitchen... and even carried on sleeping right through his own rescue, when neighbour Gary Booth carried him from his blazing house.

MAYBE IT WAS THE FAIRIES who rescued Christopher Wearstler, 21, a hiker who had been lost for nine days in Olympic State Park, Washington State, in June 1997. A search party, based at Elkhorn Ranger Station, had failed to find him, but Wearstler found them instead, walking into their camp and saying that the sound of bagpipes and flutes had led him there. He'd lost 25lb and was dehydrated, but a hospital check-up showed no injuries. Ranger Curt Sauer confessed to being puzzled by the tale of bagpipes, but had a rather more prosaic explanation. "We don't have any up there," he said, "so he was apparently beginning to hallucinate."

TWO-YEAR-OLD Sara Sullivan was saved by her grandmother Joan, 54, when a one-ton wheat-planter rolled over them in Salina, Kansas, in October 1990. Joan threw herself over her granddaughter just in time, and both managed to survive without being cut to pieces by the twisting blades. Joan was hospitalised with broken bones and bruises but Sara escaped with just a few scrapes.

CHAPTER SIX

FALLING DOWN DRUNK, literally, a 68-year-ols man slipped on the platform at Bentencho Station in Osaka, Japan, in March 1993, and started to fall into the gap between the platform-edge and a train that was just starting to pull out from the station. The driver immediately hit the brakes, but that only managed to wedge the man's head between the train and the plateform. A passenger who tried to pull the intoxicated man free gave up when he cried out in pain, but help was at hand. Some 50 passengers got together to form a rescue team, and pushed, and pushed... until they managed to tilt the train-carriage enough for the man to be freed. He escaped with minor cuts to the head and ear.

A BUNCH OF BOOMERANGS

If something truly belongs to you, it always returns in the end... even if it takes years!

JOHN GIBSON, 81, was a fighter ace in the Battle of Britain, downing 14 German aircraft during his time with 501 Squadron. When he survived being shot down in a dogfight, parachute makers Irvin presented him with an inscribed gold brooch in the shape of a caterpillar. He put it under his uniform lapel, but a fortnight later he had to bail out again, landing in the North Sea near Folkestone. When his uniform was sent for dry cleaning, it came back without the caterpillar. After the war, Gibson forgot the brooch and moved to New Zealand, only returning to England in 1989.

In 1997, he was visiting the Queen's Medical Centre in Nottingham with a friend, where they met Ivor Thomas, 75, and the conversation turned to the war. When Gibson mentioned his name, it turned out that Thomas had worked at

Eastman's dry cleaning business in Acton, and had found the caterpillar brooch in August 1940. He gave it to his mother, but it had remained in the family ever since, and was duly returned to Gibson in July 1997.

WE HAVE TALES APLENTY of lost rings returning to their rightful owners in various ways – it seems to happen all the time – so only a small selection of the more interesting ones will be given here. Brenda Rawson lost her diamond engagement ring on a beach at St Annes, Lancashire, in 1961. She and her fiancé, Christopher Firth, sifted through the sands on six successive weekends, but without success. They married the next year and continued to check with police lost-and-found files whenever they returned for holidays, but all to no avail. Then, in 1977, Christopher's uncle died, and he discovered through a solicitor that he had a long-lost cousin, John, who lived not far away from his own home in Yorkshire. In July 1979, during a conversation about metal detectors, John told Brenda that one of his children had found a diamond ring at St Annes, 18 years before. It was her ring.

WHEN HE GRADUATED from Altoona High School, near Pittsburgh, in 1965, Bob Eamigh paid $50 for a gold class ring with a red stone, engraved with the school's name and insignia, the year, and his initials, "RRE". He lost it in 1967, either at Penn State University or during training for the Vietnam war; but certainly before he went overseas. He had never been to Hawaii, either, but that's where the ring was found, in 1998, by snorkeller Ken DaVico, 62, whose hobby is finding lost objects under the sea. DaVico traced the school, and the ring was eventually returned to Eamigh through its alumni network. But there is still a stranger twist to the tale: the ring was found embedded in coral with World War II bullets and bullet casings, and a small case used by soldiers of that era to carry cigarettes. So we have two mysteries here: how did it get to Hawaii, and when did it arrive?

BACK IN 1984, Erik Jansson, 67, of Hudiksvall, Sweden, lost his distinctive gold ring, probably in the snow or on his way to his cellar. Twelve years later, he pulled up a carrot in his garden plot to give to a neighbour and, when the earth was shaken off, there was the ring. The carrot had grown straight through it. This, however, was only the end of the story. Jansson had previously lost the ring in 1982, while swimming on holiday in Sicily. The water was so deep he gave up searching, but a few hours later an amateur diver found it by chance and returned it to him. Few are the tales of rings lost and returned twice. As for the beginning of the story, who knows? Jansson found the ring himself while digging a ditch by the road in 1973. The original owner was never traced.

AFTER LOSING her opal ring in 1975, Mrs S Judges of Chatham, Kent, dreamed that it was in her chicken run. As soon as it was light, she went to the run – but found nothing. Two days later, one of the hens was killed for dinner, and there in its crop was the lost ring.

ANOTHER DREAMER with similar good luck was Paula Brine of Somerset. She lost a diamond earring on Christmas Eve 1998, but a few nights later she dreamed of seeing the earring trapped in a vanity unit in a nearby pub. She arranged for a plumber to pull up the floorboards and have a look – and, yes, the earring turned up exactly where she'd dreamed it would be.

NORMAN FLETCHER, a deckhand on a Hartlepool fishing vessel in 1975, was helping to pull in the nets, 100 miles out in the North Sea, when wind blew off his cap. It sank beneath the waves, along with his freshly-filled pipe, tucked in behind a stud. A month later, he and a mate were pulling in the nets again, at a spot about 20 miles from the first incident, when his mate extracted the cap from the net, with the pipe still in place.

WHILE SWIMMING WITH FRIENDS near Sunset Beach, North Carolina, in 1972, Ricky Shipman lost his wallet in the waters of the Atlantic when it slipped out of his swimsuit pocket. But 11 years later, his driving licence was returned to him by N C Gause, owner of a restaurant at Little River. A friend of Gause had been fishing near Sunset Beach in August 1983 and had caught a fairly large Spanish mackerel. When it was cut open, the driving licence was found inside, with Shipman's details, the photo still crystal clear because it was coated in plastic.

IN THE SUMMER of 1979, a Ukrainian woman was helping her husband set up his angling gear by the River Dnieper, when she unwittingly dropped her gold wristwatch into the water. Her husband's first catch of the day was a 7lb pike, and the watch was found still ticking in its belly.

MAKING HIS WAY out to sea in a pedalo, 150 yards from the beach of the Spanish resort of Benidorm, Bill Lees forgot that he still had his glasses on, only realising when he dived off the boat into the water, and the spectacles were lost. During the following night, though, he had a feeling that he knew exactly where they were. Next morning his daughter bought some diving goggles, they rowed out together, and she found them at the designated spot, in about 15ft of water.

THE BROTHER of Mrs E Owens of Bristol wrote to her from Canada in 1980, asking if a book of his was still at home. No sign of the volume could be found, and it was believed to have been given to a jumble sale years earlier. A week later in a second-hand bookshop, Mrs Owens spotted a copy of the book. Opening it to see the price, she found his name on the fly-leaf.

FRESH BACK FROM World War I, Gunner Tom Waterloo Dando lost his prized war medal in a mill pond at his home village of Ackworth, Yorkshire. He became a miner, married, and raised four children, but he never forgot the medal, and often went looking for it, until his death in 1942. In 1979, an elderly man knocked at the door of Tom's son, also called Tom, who was by then aged 60, and asked: "Did your father ever lose a medal?" It was, indeed, old Tom's medal, even though 60 years had passed, during which the pond had been drained after 1945, the land bulldozed, levelled, seeded and built on. Eventually, the caller's daughter had found the medal in her vegetable patch.

IT WAS THREE TIMES LUCKY for the appropriately named Dick Luck, in 1985. Luck was a 79-year-old tramp who nonetheless carried around £12,927 in his bag. He lost the bag twice, in Southampton and London, and in both places it was returned by members of the public. Eventually, he reported it missing again, having forgotten that on police advice he had put the money in a bank. When this was pointed out to him, he and his money were reunited.

HARRY WALKER, 69, of Belper in Derbyshire, tried to ring the police in February 1995 to see if there was any news of his pet falcon, Lenny, which had gone missing the day before. He misdialled, and found himself speaking to a family living several streets away from him, who told him the bird was perched on their fence.

ANOTHER FALCON TALE concerns Yaska, a three-year-old Lanner falcon owned by conservationist Eddie Hare of Tunbridge Wells. Yaska escaped when Hare tripped in July 1997. Two and half weeks later, Yaska turned up near Clitheroe, Lancashire, and was rescued by falconer Peter Wall. A few days earlier, Wall had phoned Hare, who he'd never met, to arrange to visit him. He was about to phone him to confirm the meeting, on the following day, when he was called out by a gamekeeper to deal with Yaska. When he looked at the ring on the bird's leg, he found the same phone number he was about to call anyway. Wall returned the bird to Tunbridge Wells in person the next day.

A JERSEY NIGHTCLUB was where Nick Coomes, 18, lost his watch in 1996. Two months later, on a train journey from London to his home in Salisbury, he asked a stranger the time and saw she was wearing a watch just like his. In fact, it was his. The girl had also been to the nightclub on holiday and found the watch, which was engraved with his name.

ANDY SCOTHERN lost his new camera in the mud at the Glastonbury Festival in 1997, but it was returned to him not long afterwards by Kirsty Kelly-Lewin. She had picked up the camera after losing her own in the same way, developed the film it contained, and recognised Scothern from one of the photos taken on the dance floor of a club in Nottingham.

CHAPTER EIGHT

BACK FROM THE DEAD

No, death isn't the end of everything... sometimes.

DECLARED DEAD after falling into a coma in July 1997, Abdel-Sattar Abdel-Salem Badawi, was placed in a coffin and taken to the hospital's refrigerated morgue in Menoufia, Egypt. For 12 hours he lay there, before waking up. "I opened my eyes but couldn't see anything," he said. "I moved my hands and pushed the coffin's lid to find myself among the dead." Climbing out of the coffin, he began shouting for help, and eventually three hospital employees came along to collect another body. They found him standing there, and one of the three, a paramedic, promptly collapsed with shock and died. His body was placed in the same coffin, and Badawi hurriedly left the premises.

TWO-YEAR-OLD Michael Troche wandered out of the house in Milwaukee, Wisconsin, while his parents slept, in January

1985. He was wearing only light pyjamas, and the temperature outside had plummeted to a record low of minus 16 degrees centigrade. Michael soon collapsed in the snow, and when his father found him several hours later he was literally frozen stiff. His limbs had hardened, ice crystals had formed both on and below his skin, and he had stopped breathing for an unknown length of time. He was rushed to the city's Children's Hospital, where he was described as "dead, extremely dead," but 18 doctors and 20 nurses set to work on him for six hours. Ice crystals in his body were heard cracking as he was lifted onto the operating table. His blood was warmed in a heart-lung machine, and as his body thawed, drugs were used to prevent his brain swelling. His arms and legs did swell, however, as fluid leaked from ice-damaged cells, and incisions had to be made to allow the tissues to expand.

Michael remained semi-conscious for three days, then made a rapid recovery. There was minor damage to his left hand, and he needed skin grafts to cover the incisions, but he avoided brain damage. This was attributed to the wind-chill factor, which effectively quick-froze him so rapidly that his metabolism had very little demand for oxygen.

ALSO IN WISCONSIN, 57-year-old taxidermist David Kostichka of Forestville was found slumped in an armchair in March 1985, when his brother and a neighbour broke into his house to investigate his 'disappearance'. He had been sitting there, unconscious, for seven days after a shot through a window lodged a bullet in his head. He was also suffering from hypothermia, malnutrition and dehydration, but survived because the unheated house kept his body temperature low.

TWENTY MINUTES under the icy waters of Lake Michigan should have killed off four-year-old Jimmy Tontlewicz in

January 1984, and he was, indeed, pronounced dead on arrival at the Children's Memorial Hospital in Chicago. He had been sledging on the lake-front when the ice gave way, plunging him into the freezing water. Rather than try to revive him immediately, doctors kept him in a drug-induced coma to control his brain pressure. A week on, he was said to have recovered well without obvious signs of brain damage, although a year later he was still receiving treatment for "a minor speech problem." Hypothermia expert Dr Robert Pozos explained that the smaller you are, and the faster you're chilled, the better your chances for survival.

STORM CLOUDS GATHERED over Hanston, Kansas, in August 1901, as a horse-drawn hearse led a solemn procession to the cemetery. In a metallic coffin within the hearse lay the body of the five-year-old daughter of a local farmer, Samuel McPreaz. As the sky darkened, mourners noticed a "peculiar, soft mellow light" in the sky. Then there was a clap of thunder and the hearse was struck by lightning. The bolt knocked down both horses, stunned the driver and burst open the coffin. Mourners found the 'dead' girl sitting up, crying for her mother. Doctors supposed the girl was in a cataleptic condition and that the shock revived her. Her parents and other locals, however, believed she was dead, and that her return to life was miraculous... a belief bolstered by the fact that no-one was seriously injured by the lightning bolt.

HER FAMILY were hardly shocked when Kalenben Balabhai died in January 1989; she had reached the age of 100 after all. They took her to the cremation ground in Malanka village, near Rajkot, in Gujurat, India, and placed her on the pyre. As relatives prepared to send her off in flames, the 'dead' woman sat up and demanded to be taken home. There she found that her son Luxan had let her flat to Amuan and Selim Kahaan. Being dead obviously hadn't improved the old woman's temper, because she flew into a rage and threw some of the Kahaans' furniture out of the windows before calling the police.

IN ROMANIA, a man named only as Neagu, 71, collapsed coughing after swallowing a fishbone in 1991, and apparently stopped breathing. The family doctor, who knew he had a bad heart, confirmed that he had died of a heart attack. Three days after he was buried, gravediggers at the cemetery heard him knocking and found him lying in the coffin among wilted flowers.

When he returned home, his wife opened the door and promptly fainted; she and her children thereafter refused to have anything to do with him, apparently fearing that he was a ghost. It took Neagu three weeks to persuade police, town hall officials, doctors and priests to erase his death from their registers.

AN OMANI WOMAN from Liwa province had apparently died in 1990 after a long coma, and was being prepared for burial. As her son splashed her with water as part of traditional Muslim rites, she sat up and shouted: "I'm still alive!"

DURING THE BURIAL SERVICE in Longano, northern Italy, the 'deceased', Ernesto Quirino, 60, opened his eyes, looked round in horror, leapt out of the coffin and made a run for it. He collapsed after 100 yards, but after a check-up by a doctor was found to be well.

UNEXPECTED PERILS sometimes await foreign travellers. Steve Castledene, 39, was teaching English in Bangkok, Thailand, in 1991, when he was knocked off his motorbike. He was picked up by a pirate ambulance crew who eavesdrop on emergency radios, arrive first at the site of the crash, and make fast money charging accident victims for their services. Castledene was unconscious and covered in mud and blood from headwounds, but the untrained ambulancemen thought he was dead and dumped him at the city morgue. He woke up an hour later, crammed in between other corpses.

UNPLEASANT THINGS seem to happen sometimes in Romania. An 18-year-old girl, declared clinically dead in 1992, regained consciousness while being raped on a slab by a necrophiliac mortuary attendant in Bucharest. Police arrested the shocked rapist, but the parents refused to press charges because their daughter "owed her life to him."

WHEN A TYRE BURST in 1977, the hearse carrying Gerry Allison to his funeral on the outskirts of Los Angeles overturned and crashed tail-first into the front window of a rival undertaker's parlour. The hearse doors burst open and flung the coffin through the window. Bystanders were astonished to see Allison, dressed in white burial robes, step out of the shattered glass. The crash had brought him out of a coma that doctors had mistaken for death.

HENRY LODGE, 63, had a heart attack in June 1986 while fixing fuses. Declared dead, he was about to be dissected by Dr Phillip Campbell in the Los Angeles mortuary when he opened his eyes and yelled for help. The 'dead' ended up better off than the doctor: Lodge was duly sent home, but Campbell took an extended leave suffering from nervous exhaustion.

FORMER CRANE DRIVER Mrs Yuliya Vorobyeva was pronounced dead at the age of 37 and spent two nights in a mortuary after receiving a 380-volt electric shock in a mine near Donetsk, Ukraine, in March 1978. A doctor and his assistant began an autopsy, but with the first cut blood started to pump out and she began to shake.

After that the story gets stranger. Mrs Vorobyeva didn't sleep for six months after her revival, then fell into a long sleep. When she woke up again, she found she had some sort of X-ray vision, could see diseased organs in people, predict storms and see through asphalt roads. She apparently went on to make a new career as a medical consultant.

AFTER A CAR SMASH near Vereeniging, South Africa, in March 1993, Sipho William Mdletshe, 24, from Sebokeng township, was declared dead and taken to a mortuary. He spent two days in a metal box, drifting in and out of consciousness, then slowly became alert enough to realise he was trapped, and began screaming for help. Mortuary workers heard the commotion and freed him. Unfortunately his fiancée, Keidibone, who was also injured in the crash, refused to believe his story. She told nurses at the hospital where she was recuperating that he was a zombie returned from the dead to haunt her.

IN MARCH 1995, the body of suspected thief Mvuyisi Mcetywa was taken to a government mortuary in Umtata, Transkei, in South Africa. He regained consciousness just before he was about to be refrigerated, and lived to accuse three policemen of torturing him.

POLICE ARRESTED Peter Archer, 47, for running naked down the street in Melbourne, Australia, in March 1996. He was released, however, when it was discovered that he was fleeing from a mortuary where a doctor had pronounced him dead.

TWO MORGUE ATTENDANTS in Havana, Cuba, playing chess on the night shift to pass the time, got the shock of their lives in October 1996. One of the 'corpses' suddenly sat up, reached over and moved one of the chessmen. Miguel Garcia had suffered a heart attack and been pronounced dead, but came to on the slab. Disoriented, he grabbed the first thing he saw – the black bishop. He moved it three squares and dropped it. Garcia later recovered in the Havana General Hospital, but how his move affected the chess game isn't known.

AN OLD LADY of 86 lay for five-and-a-half months in an "irreversible" coma in Albany, New York, following a stroke. Mrs Carrie Coons had told friends for years that she didn't wish to be kept alive by artificial means, so her 88-year-old sister brought a landmark court case in April 1989, which led to the removal of the feeding tubes which had been keeping her alive. Five days later, Mrs Coons woke up, and began talking and eating strained baby food. Rather pointlessly, the Supreme Court judge who had sanctioned her 'death' then reversed his order.

ONE OF THE MOST BIZARRE tales of revival comes from Aseer in southern Saudi Arabia. Muattak Zafer Al-Shaani, 49, was fixing a windmill when one of the vanes knocked him unconscious. When his family failed to revive him, they thought he was dead and buried him. About 27 hours later, he woke to the sound of hooves as grazing sheep walked over his grave. Shepherds heard his screams and dug him up, and he walked home in his burial shroud. Although the story couldn't be officially corroborated, various newspaper sources say that when his mother and sister saw him, "they went mad and dropped dead". Others add that he went mad as well, and was sent to an asylum. Perhaps it wasn't his lucky day after all.

WHAT DREAMS MAY COME

Lucky escapes and great good fortune...
foretold by dreams and premonitions.

IN THAILAND, 27-year-old food-seller Praiwan Sahib moved to Bangkok, hoping to support her children after a drought destroyed her husband's rice crop. Then she dreamed that unhappy ghosts appeared and begged her to help their impoverished souls in the underworld. She replied that she couldn't help because she had no money to buy merit for their souls, and the ghosts promised to give her a fortune. They gave her lottery numbers, and the following morning she spent her last £2.50 on two tickets. The numbers came up, winning her £150,000, and Ms Praiwan just as promptly fainted. She did, though, make swift offerings to her ghostly benefactors.

MARIA TEJADA was watching television at her home in Kissimmee, Florida, in February 1999, when she heard the voice of her father, who had died five years earlier, telling her to get off the couch. "I didn't listen the first two times he said it, but the third time I got up and went over to the love seat," she said later. As she moved, a car carrying two teenagers on their way to school crashed through the front door, knocked over the couch where she had been sitting, and demolished an interior wall. Father, it seems, really does know better – even from beyond the grave.

SHOP-GIRL MARY REDDING, 24, of Stirchley, Birmingham, dreamed she was going to win the football pools. In spite of the fact that most books of dream-interpretation will tell you that to dream of winning at gambling actually means the opposite and indicates loss or lack of success, five days later Mary picked up a cheque for £132,631 from Vernon's pools.

SOMETHING ROUSED Mrs Noreen Croasdale from her sleep in January 1974, at her house in Accrington, Lancashire. Then she heard a creaking noise and woke her husband. They went outside and saw cracks and a big hole in the wall, so they dashed back inside and grabbed their four children. Seconds after the family had got out into the street, their luck ran out: the house collapsed, destroying all their possessions.

A LUCKY ESCAPE for Byrnice Whaley of Cockenzie, East Lothian. Her mother Frances dreamed that Byrnice had toothache, and when she phoned around she found a dentist in Musselburgh who could treat her. Arriving, in the dream, she found the place was an old house with an ornate ceiling in the waiting room. When she took Byrnice to the toilet, she noticed black-and-white 'chessboard' lino on the floor, then returned to the waiting room while Byrnice went into the surgery. A friend came in and they chatted, until the dentist appeared and said: "I'm sorry, but your daughter has died under gas". Mrs Whaley woke up sobbing, but forgot the dream until months later.

Then Byrnice woke up with a terrible toothache. Mrs Whaley phoned around, and the only dentist who could give her a quick appointment was in Musselburgh. It turned out to be an old house; the waiting room had an ornate ceiling, the toilet black-and-white lino. A friend came in and started chatting, and she realised her dream was coming true. Then the door opened, and the dentist said: "I'm sorry... I can't take out Byrnice's tooth. She's got a cold." Not surprisingly, Mrs Whaley grabbed Byrnice and fled, although why she'd waited that long is something of a puzzle in itself. The tooth was taken out two days later by another dentist.

NURSE'S AIDE Pearl Anderson, 54, of Oakland, California, had a dream about money gushing from a slot machine. She woke up and drove straight to Reno, Nevada, going to the slot machines at 2:00am. On her second try at the $3 "millionaire slot machine", five sevens appeared, winning one million dollars. It was the largest payout from the machine since it had been installed three years earlier.

A YOUNG MARE called Unni escaped from her field in Öster-bymo, Sweden, in July 1995. Her owner, 19-year-old Ingela Gustavsson, searched the nearby forest for weeks with no luck, and neither the police nor advertisements in the local paper brought any news. Then, six weeks after the escape, Ingela woke at four in the morning after a dream in which she'd seen Unni grazing at a megalithic monument called the Dackestenar, in a forest two kilometres from her home. She phoned her boyfriend, who was sceptical but agreed to accompany her to the stones, where they immediately saw evidence that a horse had been there. Unni was found on a path nearby, rather wild and very thin – but not so wild that a bucket of oats couldn't persuade her to return to civilisation.

ANTHEA SLATER was about to change baby Luke's nappy on the kitchen table as usual, in November 1985, when she suddenly felt an inexplicable compulsion to take him into the living room and do the deed there instead. Only a minute later, a lorry crashed through the garden fence of her house in Bath and overturned, spilling its load of 12 tons of gravel. The gravel smashed through the kitchen window, wrecking the place and burying the table where the baby would have been lying.

WAKING SUDDENLY from an afternoon nap in his vicarage in Austria, Father Stanislaw Wenerski jumped up and yelled: "Quick! Get everybody out!" He hustled his housekeeper out into the street, then dashed into the 200-year-old church of St Jakob's next door. It took a few minutes to usher out the worshippers and his fellow priests and then, almost immediately afterwards, both church and vicarage collapsed into a heap of rubble. Investigations showed that both buildings had been put up over a cave, part of an ancient brickworks that nobody knew existed.

TROUBLED BY ARTHRITIS, 76-year-old Ivy Jones of Walsall dreamed that she could cure herself by keeping elephant dung in her bra. She wrote to Dudley Zoo who, perhaps surprisingly, provided her with some pachyderm poop and, yes, it worked! The crapulous cure brought movement back to her shoulder.

BUSILY PREPARING DINNER in the kitchen of her new home in Witzhelden, Germany, housewife Margaret Woellner was surprised when her 10-year-old son Joachim suddenly burst in. Obviously terrified, he stood in the doorway and said: "Mummy, get out of the kitchen quickly... something terrible is going to happen!" Looking at his ashen face, Mrs Woellner realised he wasn't joking, so she scooped up her 3-year-old daughter Ulrike and together they dashed out of the house. Seconds later an explosion, caused by a faulty gas-main connection, wrecked the three-bedroom house. Asked how he knew the accident was about to happen, Joachim replied: "I honestly don't know. I just had this strange idea that something was about to happen. It was as if there was a voice saying 'Go and fetch your mother and sister otherwise it will be too late'."

WONDERING WHY her 18-year-old son Clive was late home for supper, Mrs Doris Ingle of Blackpool had a 'hunch' that he was still at the bank where he worked. But something still worried her, so she called the police, who in turn contacted the branch manager. Then Mrs Ingle made the unlikely suggestion of checking the vault, where they found both Clive and Stephen Goodall, 17. They had been trapped in the vault for seven hours, having gone in at the end of the day to fetch something. The door had been closed on them, and they hadn't been missed as the bank was closed up straight afterwards.

CUTLERY POLISHER Paula Smith had a strange premonition that her grandfather Charlie Watson was in danger, in February 1986. It was so strong, in fact, that she left her factory bench and raced home, to find Charlie, who should have been celebrating his 63rd birthday, lying on the floor gasping for breath. She called an ambulance and he was rushed to hospital, where he was treated for a perforated ulcer.

CLAIRVOYANCE features in our next tale, rather than a premonition. Ismael Aldana's two children were aboard a plane that crashed in a remote jungle area of north-west Colombia in April 1997, but the plane couldn't be located. Just as rescuers were about to give up the search, Aldana consulted a local sorceress, and she told him where they should be looking. The crashed plane was located near the town she named, and the two children were found alive.

WIDOWER FRED JONES, 62, from Crewe, thought afterwards that it might have been a premonition that made his friends persuade him to stay the night when he went to visit them, in March 1986. It was the first time in his life, apparently, that he'd ever stayed away from home for the night. When he walked home the following morning, his house wasn't there any more. It had been destroyed in a gas explosion, and police, firemen and neighbours were frantically searching the rubble for his body. The blast had shattered windows 300 yards away, but the clock on Jones' mantelpiece was still ticking. Obviously his time wasn't up.

LAND OF THE LOST

The family that strays together, stays together...
when they eventually find each other again.

CAR WORKSHOP MANAGER Philip Yeomans, 42, was born in Wexford, Ireland, and brought up by his aunt after his father died and his mother had a nervous breakdown. His aunt died in 1975, and he spent the next 22 years and £5,000 travelling 20,000 miles in search of relatives, even placing an appeal on an ITV Teletext service. By October 1997 he was living in Paignton, Devon, and his girlfriend Judith Woodward mentioned his quest to Mary Sammons, 52, a fellow care assistant at the nursing home where she worked. Mrs Sammons, a mother of six, realised that she was his sister, and the pair were finally reunited.

WORKING AT Airlynx Airport Services in Southampton in April 1997, Mrs Lesley Bailey noticed that John Leadbitter, 49, looked very much like her husband, Peter. She knew that her husband's surname had been Leadbitter before he was adopted as a toddler and separated from his family, so she asked the man, who had come in to book transport for a holiday, if he had a brother called Peter. John looked at her, completely stunned, and then broke down in tears. He lived with his wife in Swaything, Southampton, while the Baileys lived only a mile away in the Bitterne area, and John had been trying to find his brother for years. It turned out that they had grown up in villages near Southampton only a mile apart, had attended the same school and shared many friends without realising they were related.

PETER AND JENNY STANTON were separated when they went to different foster homes in 1940. Peter began searching for his sister in 1964, but it was only in March 1996 that he struck lucky. Jenny Fletcher, 57, had been living for the previous nine years in Blackwell, near Bromsgrove, Worcestershire, only three miles from Peter's home in Rednal. Two of their children, Peter's son Gary and Jenny's daughter Jaqui, had dated each other as teenagers, unaware of the family link, and Mr Stanton had, on one occasion, driven to his sister's home to drop Gary off. He also discovered that he'd worked on the same car factory production line as his sister's husband. Eventually reunited, they prepared to catch up on their lost years, and get to know each other's children, seven in total.

SEPARATED FROM his unmarried mother when he was six, Michael Drennen, 34, had been searching for her for years. In March 1992, he was in a video store in York, Nebraska, when he overheard Mrs Shirley Keener give her maiden name to a clerk, and realised his search was over. Mrs Keener, then 59, had her four children, aged six, five, three and two, taken away from her by county officials in February 1964 because she was unmarried. Both she and her son had lived in York since 1990.

BECAUSE HER MOTHER was an alcoholic, Tammy Harris was adopted at the age of two. But after her 21st birthday in March 1990, she began searching for her mother. The following February, she mentioned her search to a colleague at the Stop In convenience store where she worked in Roanoke, Virginia. When she produced her birth certificate, Mrs Joyce Shultz, the woman she had been working alongside for the last six months, realised that this was the daughter she had been trying to find for 20 years. She kept her secret for three days because she wasn't sure how her daughter would react, but everything worked out fine. They had lived only two streets apart for the previous two years.

BLIND EX-GUNNER Ray Ackroyd, 87, had lost touch with his adopted sons, Rod and Shankill Davis, 30 years before, but longed to meet them again before he died. Ray and his late wife Mary had adopted the orphans when his regiment was stationed in Wales in 1942, and in 1991 he saved his pension money and hired a taxi to drive him from his home in Winston, Co. Durham, 250 miles to Aberaeron, near Aberystwyth, where he had last heard of them living. Arriving there, the cabbie flagged down a passing car and asked the driver if he knew Rod Davis. The man replied: "I'm Rod Davis." Soon afterwards, Ray was reunited with Shankill as well.

MYRA MURRAY of Huntingdon phoned a friend who lived on a farm in North Yorkshire in 1985. The friend answered the phone, but what she said made no apparent sense: "I'm sorry, but Hilary is out for the evening." It turned out that the friend was not at home, but out baby-sitting at a farm two miles away. Miss Murray had no idea who Hilary was, or where the farm was situated; she'd dialled the wrong number, but got the right friend.

KNOWING SHE WAS the offspring of a war-time love-affair, Vivien Fletoridis had been adopted in 1941 and went to Australia with her adoptive parents in 1954. There she married, and had two children who had grown up by 1987, when she decided to travel 13,000 miles back to England to track down her family. Her mother had died in 1983, but she traced her brothers and sisters through an agency, then set off in search of her father.

In a library in Southport she was looking through an electoral roll when an old man asked her if she was going to be long; she replied that she was looking for a man called Hewitt. The old man, of course, turned out to be Wilf Hewitt, 86, the father she hadn't seen for 46 years.

RECEIVING A LETTER from his long-lost mother Brenda in 1995, Tony Munden discovered that he had two half-sisters. Brenda, 47, had split up with Tony's father when he was 18 months old, and later emigrated to South Africa with her two daughters, Lorraine and Paula, from a second failed marriage. She had written from Johannesburg, where she was living with Paula and her third husband. Tony, a 26-year-old labourer from Weston-super-Mare, had fended for himself since he his father left him when he was ten, and now decided to try to find his half-sister Lorraine. He discovered her living next door, their bedroom windows facing each other only 15 feet apart. They had been neighbours for three months without knowing of each other's existence.

WHEN TINA DIXON was adopted in 1961, her two brothers were adopted into another family. She knew that one had kept his original name, Innes, while the other took that of his adoptive family, Brown, but despite all her efforts she had failed to trace them. Mrs Dixon, a hairdresser from Stocksfield,

Northumberland, and her husband decided to enter a pairs golf competition at Hexham in November 1996, and found themselves matched against Mark Innes and Ron Wingfield. When Mrs Dixon pulled a shoulder muscle on the tenth tee, it was suggested she should see Mark's brother, a physiotherapist. When told that his name was Kevin Brown, she realised that she'd found her brothers and, following a phone call and a hectic 50-mile drive by Kevin, the siblings were reunited.

PERHAPS NOT SO LUCKY after all, was a robber who was jailed for eight years in Argentina and hired a detective to trace the father he had never met only to discover he was the warder of his prison.

JOIE GIESE and Merrilee Woeber worked together for three years at MCI Telecommunications in Davenport, Iowa, and in May 1997 a co-worker suggested that Giese might be Italian, because of her olive skin. "Not me, I was a Dunn," replied Giese, 51. "I must be Irish." Woeber, 50, added that she was a Dunn as well. Giese said that her mother was Lenore Dunn, who had died in 1962, and the pair realised they were half-sisters. Giese's father was unknown, and she had been adopted, while Woeber was the offspring of Lenore and her husband, Chester Anderson, who had died in 1974.

FINALLY, TWO TALES of people who simply got lost. Collecting logs with his son-in-law, John Johnson, 69, of Pembina, North Dakota, went astray in dense woods near the Canadian border, in May 1998. He was lost for eight days, before making his way to a road, where he was found by a couple driving by in a car, and taken to hospital. He had survived by eating lily-pad roots.

FAR MORE STARTLING was the survival of Li Qingzhu, 16, who was one of four girls who got lost in a cave in Guizhou province, south-west China, at the same time as Johnson, in May 1998. Plunged into darkness when their candle went out and completely without food, two of the girls died before they could be found... but Li and Liang Xiaofei, 19, survived for 42 days before being brought to the surface. Sadly, Liang died two days later in hospital, but when last heard of, Li was still alive.

WHAT'S UP, DOC?

A few tales of the human condition – the human medical condition, that is.

A PLASTIC TOY STETHOSCOPE saved the life of accountant Terry Killeavy, 36, from Gotham, Nottinghamshire, in October 1998. He won it as a joke prize in a darts match at his local pub. On the way home, he put it to his chest and realised that something was wrong. His heart was beating eight or nine times and then stopping, to be followed by a double beat. He hurried to his GP and was referred to the Nuffield Hospital in Leicester, where he was given emergency surgery for a hole in his heart the size of a 50p coin. Mr Killeavy's brother haD died in 1984, aged 23, from a heart defect which had gone undetected, and he firmly believed he owed his life to the toy stethoscope.

A BLOW TO THE HEAD from a cricket ball put Robert Newham, a 36-year-old policeman from Elston, Nottinghamshire, into a coma for three days in 1998. Luckily, though, he was given a brain scan as a result, and that revealed a dangerous tangle of weakened arteries in his brain that would have been fatal in 10 to 15 years. Doctors were confident that radio-therapy would cure the arterio-venous malformation, which may have developed from an abnormality at birth.

A TEENAGER, identified only as VJ, was stabbed in a fight in Esztergom, Hungary, in 1997. Doctors expected the 18-year-old to die, as the knife had apparently penetrated his heart. VJ was luckier than that, however: his heart was on the right hand side, the blade had just missed it, and he recovered from his wounds.

CLUB DOORMAN Murray Atwell, 31, from Dunster, Somerset, had a lifelong stammer. Then, in 1997, his four-year-old son Connery, using a broom handle as a 'hockey stick', playfully bopped him over the head. The blow knocked him flat and made him dizzy. As his wife was away, it wasn't until the next day, when he chatted with his mother, that he realised that the blow had cured him of his stammer.

LAWYER MARY DIGNAN was hurrying to a hearing in Sacramento, California, in July 1997, obviously with other things in her head than looking at the train which hit her and knocked her unconscious. When she underwent a preliminary brainscan at the Davis Medical Center, one of the things that was found was a brain tumour. Doctors said the prognosis was good because they had found the tumour early.

RETIRED BUSINESSMAN Klaus Schmidt, 64, was on a Lufthansa flight from Dublin to Frankfurt in 1998, when he suffered serious heart problems and had difficulty breathing, at 11,000ft. The chief steward asked if there was a doctor on board, and was met with 40 raised arms from the entire German delegation to an international medical seminar in

Ireland. Many were carrying newly-developed heart-drugs in their hand-luggage. A professor from Heidelberg loosened Mr Schmidt's collar, while a specialist in microscopic surgery gave him an injection. Within minutes, the colour returned to his cheeks and he was breathing more easily, and he was able to walk from the plane when it landed, with some help. "I was lucky to choose the right flight," he told a stewardess. "I'd been thinking of flying back the next day and then changed my mind."

DEAF-MUTE Truong Van Xa, 32, had an operation on a foot abscess in 1998, and found the pain so great that he spoke for the first time. He had received a local anæsthetic for the operation, at Binh Dinh provincial hospital in Vietnam, but when Dr Vo Thanh Nhan made the first incision, he screamed "painful!" His vocabulary has grown since, but his hearing is still impaired.

A STEAM RALLY at East Grinstead, Sussex, had obviously branched out into other things apart from old tractors, in August 1977. One of the attractions was a model aircraft flying display, which was being watched by Andy Knapp when one of the planes suddenly dive-bombed him at 60 mph, and hit him in the neck. He stopped breathing, but was saved by another odd attraction. Nearby, a doctor was demonstrating a mobile heart resuscitator and he instantly connected Knapp to the machine and saved his life.

ALEXANDRA CHAMBERS, 16, of Billericay, Essex, fell off a rope swing into a ditch, in May 1994. She scrambled out, walked half a mile home, touched her toes "to see if anything was broken", and let her mother massage her neck. It was only when her wrist started to hurt that her father took her to hospital in Basildon, where it was discovered that she had broken her neck in four places. She was immediately transferred to the specialist unit at Stoke Mandeville Hospital where she spent six weeks recovering, with her head in total stasis; even a movement of half an inch, doctors said, could have caused death or paralysis.

A CANADIAN MAN of 19, named only as 'George', suffered for years from a compulsion to take four-hour showers and to wash his hands up to 50 times a day. He also had an extreme fear of bacteria, and was constantly checking to see if doors and windows were locked. He had to leave school, and constantly spoke about suicide. Finally, taunted by his mother (who may, perhaps understandably, have had enough), he took a .22 calibre pistol and shot himself in the mouth. Instead of killing himself, though, he performed a precise operation on the left frontal lobe of his brain. Surgeons removed the slug, though they couldn't get out all the fragments, and his ritualistic behaviour became much less pronounced, while his IQ remained unimpaired. His psychiatrist, Dr Leslie Solyom of Vancouver, British Columbia, described it as the first case of self-lobotomy he had ever heard of.

PAULA DIXON, 39, was due to fly from Hong Kong to London in May 1995, but broke her ribs in a motorcycle accident on the way to the airport. She boarded the plane anyway, but while it was in flight her lung collapsed and she became critically ill. Fortunately there were two doctors on the flight, who carried out an impromptu operation to drain her lung... using a wire coat-hanger, a rubber tube and a water bottle, along with a bottle of brandy to sterilise the equipment. The operation saved her life, and kept her in good enough shape until she could receive proper hospital treatment in London.

PLUMMETS

It isn't the fall that kills you, they say... it's when you hit the ground. But that's not always the case, as shown by these tales of terrified tumblers.

CHRIS SAGGERS, 26, plunged 22 floors (220 feet) from a tower block in Salford, in April 1993. Security videos caught his fall, estimated at around 80 mph, before he landed on the roof of a Nissan Micra car, which completely caved in. After 15 seconds he got up and walked away, telling passersby that he felt 'fine'. He was later treated for cuts, a neck injury and a suspected broken elbow. He said he was not trying to commit suicide, but had tripped on the stairs and fallen out of a window.

THE YOUNGER YOU ARE, the softer you fall, it seems. In 1997, three-year-old Lau Tim fell 13 floors from a block of flats in Hong Kong, but escaped with no more than minor fractures to her shoulder. Her fall was broken by the multitudinous clothes lines that stretch between apartment blocks there, and she landed on a corrugated iron canopy on the first floor.

EVEN YOUNGER, though, was an unnamed 18-month-old baby who plunged from a seventh floor apartment in Murcia, Spain, in November 1997. The baby's fall was also partially broken by laundry lines, but the fall's end was alarming: it ended up hurtling through the glass panes that covered the ground floor of the building. The only damage was a broken tooth, a contusion to the upper lip, and bruises on the right cheek. After a check-up by a pædiatrician, the baby was sent home.

SOME KIDS, it seems, just can't get enough of this sort of thing. Ionut Ilie, six, fell from the fourth floor of a block of flats in Iasi in Romania in 1998, escaping with slight injuries. He'd had practise at this before, having done the same at the age of one, but that time he'd only fallen from the first floor.

WINDOW CLEANER Kerry Burton, 27, almost kicked the bucket when he fell five storeys in Calgary, Alberta, after his rope mechanism failed. Fortunately, it was a bucket that saved his life – it was full of water and strapped to his backside. He landed bucket-first and then bounced about two feet back up in the air, but he survived.

THE NAME OF THE GAME is... fat. A 15-stone woman plunged 17 storeys in New York, in 1978, and crashed into, and mostly through, a parked car. Her bulk saved her, and she was pulled from the wreckage alive. Her name – Victoria Lard.

A STRANGE TALE from the Persian Gulf: in December 1980 a Saudi Arabian Airways Tristar took off from Dharhan in Saudi Arabia, heading for Karachi, in Pakistan. Going home aboard the flight were hospital technician Ziauddin Khatoon, his wife Anna, and their children, daughter Samina, 10, and son Ahmed, six. At 29,000 feet, a tyre burst in one of the wheel-wells in the plane's belly, and the blast tore a hole about two-and-a-half feet wide in the underside of the passenger compartment. The sudden decompression sucked the children out into the night. The plane made an emergency landing in Qatar, and although a search was made for the children, there was no sign of them.

Three years later, a Pakistani visiting the port of Abu Dhabi saw the two children, and the girl told him how they had been found by an Arab fisherman floating in the water and that, thinking they had dropped from heaven, he had taken them home and raised them as his own. By the time attempts were made to check, though, the fisherman had sailed on leaving the story to tail off in question marks...

ONE OF THOSE good-luck/bad-luck stories comes from the old Soviet Union, although the tale didn't emerge until nine years after the event. Mrs Larisa Savitska survived a three-mile fall from an Antonov airliner after it collided with a military aircraft near the Soviet-Chinese border in 1981. The story lacks details, but it seems she was the only survivor. After that her luck changed. She received only 75 roubles (£75) compensation (some sources say only £25) and that was for her lost luggage, rather than her injuries. Worse, she then found that she had to travel frequently to either Moscow or Vladivostok for follow-up medical treatment – at her own expense.

MONICA SCHWALEN, 20, was a Swiss skydiving instructor and veteran of more than 80 jumps. In 1990, she started a free-fall dive from a plane two miles above Sitterdorf. After 5,900 feet she forgot her own instructions and pulled the rip-cord too quickly, at which point both her main and back-up parachutes became entangled. She landed in an apple tree in a cow field at 112 mph, but survived with a broken pelvis and thigh. From her hospital bed, she remarked that she would not be giving up parachuting.

A SIMILAR ACCIDENT befell Klint Freemantle, 22, of Napier, New Zealand, in July 1993. Skydiving above Napier airport, and in full view of his relatives, he fell 3,600 feet when his main and reserve chutes became entangled. He landed in a three-feet deep pond, scattering the resident ducks, and clambered out with only a cut above one eye. The first thing he did was stand up and shout "Yes!", after which he began reeling his chutes in. He was reported to have said that he would be back skydiving just as soon as his knees stopped trembling.

PERHAPS THE STRANGEST REACTION to such an accident, though, came from Sharon McClelland, 26, who was making only her second parachute jump, and her first freefall, near Queensville, Ontario, in 1994. Her main chute failed to open properly and, forgetting the usual procedure, she failed to open the backup chute. She plummeted 10,000 feet and landed on her back in a marsh, uninjured apart from some bruising. Almost at once, she got up and apologised to her skydiving instructor.

CLEARLY DEPRESSED and drunk besides, an unnamed Brighton man decided to commit suicide by jumping off a 90-foot cliff at Telscombe, Sussex, in 1990. A passerby called the police, who tried to talk the 27-year-old man down for over an hour but he jumped anyway. A doctor was sent to the foot of the cliff to examine the body, but found the man unscratched. He then got up and walked back up to the cliff top unaided.

IN BNAI BRAK, in Israel, an unnamed 45-year-old man tried to commit suicide in 1993 by leaping from a pedestrian footbridge onto a busy highway, at the height of the midday rush hour. He landed in a truckload of mattresses and suffered only minor bruises.

A GUST OF WIND blew Aimé Grosjean, 72, off the balcony of a 17th-floor apartment in Regensdorf, Switzerland, in 1995. But what the wind takes away, it can also bring back. Another gust of wind blew him onto the balcony of the 16th-floor apartment below, the tenants of which were away at the time. The shaken pensioner landed safely, and suffered no more than bruises and a cut on his arm.

A SIX-YEAR-OLD GIRL was thrown from a fourth-floor balcony in Moscow by her suicidal mother, Irina Smirnova, 40, in 1997. A neighbour, though, ran onto his balcony and caught the child; his name, appropriately, was Gocha Laoshvili. When police tried to enter the unemployed mother's flat, however, she jumped to her death.

A PAINFUL TALE comes from Palma, Spain, where an unnamed tourist fell 65 feet from a wall in May 1991. His life was saved because he landed on a giant cactus, which broke his fall but, we're told, it took two hours to disentangle him from the plant, and another three hours to remove all the thorns.

A STURDY PAIR of jeans saved the life of Derek Boyce, 20, in April 1992. He got stuck between floors in a broken lift in an Edinburgh tower-block and, rather than wait for assistance, he decided to clamber out through an emergency hatch. Another lift passed by and sent him hurtling down the shaft, but his jeans snagged on a protruding stancheon, 10 storeys above the ground. Although his cries for help alerted other residents, he had to hang head down for more than an hour before rescuers reached him and freed him. He was taken to hospital with head and leg injuries.

IT'S ALWAYS THE SAME – there you are enjoying a nice relaxing bath when the neighbours pop in. The story had a different twist in Hong Kong in June 1990, though, when an unnamed woman fell from the window of her third-floor apartment, and hit a ledge 10 feet below. She bounced, and was catapulted sideways through an open bathroom window. She survived the ordeal okay – but what the man who was lying in the bath at the time had to say about his unexpected guest isn't recorded.

CHAPTER THIRTEEN

ALL AT SEA

A life on the ocean waves... sometimes makes you want
to get back to shore as soon as possible!

SIX REFUGEES fleeing Cuba on a raft one night in August
1994 lost their lantern overboard, and had no light by which to
read their compass. Which way was north and the USA? One
of the rafters, however, had a small good-luck companion in
his pocket... a firefly. Placing it on the compass, he found it gave
just enough light to find north, thus enabling them to turn the
raft around. Otherwise they would have been heading back
toward Cuba. All eventually arrived safely in Florida, including
the firefly though their little saviour died shortly afterwards.

A CYCLONE struck Nikunau, one of the coral atolls of the
South Pacific state of Kiribati, in November 1991, and swept a
dinghy containing three fishermen out to sea. Arenta
Tebeitabu, 40, Tabwai Mikaie, 24, and Nweiti Tekamangu, 47,
lost their outboard motor when the 13 foot dinghy capsized,

though they managed to right the craft, salvaging a spear, a fishing line and a small basin, before drifting further out to sea.

For 175 days they drifted round the South Pacific, using the spear and line to catch fish, including 10 sharks, and the basin to catch rainwater. Occasionally, a floating coconut added to their diet. Finally, 900 miles south-east of their starting point, the boat washed up on a beach in Western Samoa. Tekamangu had died a few days previously, and the other two were no more than skin and bone, too weak to walk. But somehow they managed to steer the boat past a dangerous reef before collapsing into unconsciousness. The survivors believed that the spirit of their dead comrade, whose body had been put overboard, pushed them to shore.

PERHAPS KIRIBATI FISHERMEN have strange powers, because we have another tale of three men in a boat from the same area. In April 1986, Take Taka, Tatiete Kannangaki and Bakatarawa Labo were within sight of their home village when their engine broke down, and they drifted for 119 days to Naurui, 430 miles away. They caught 25 sharks with their bare hands, clubbing them to death, drinking their blood and eating them raw. One Saturday night, however, they were praying for a different kind of fish, being sick and tired of shark, when a rare black fish suddenly fell into the 16-foot open boat. This was a fish that normally lives 620 feet down, never comes to the surface, and can't even be caught by trawling. Astonishment swiftly gave way to hunger, though, and dinner was served!

AN ODDER DIET for six Filipino fishermen who survived for 34 days after a shipwreck before being rescued near Taiwan. A storm capsized their boat near Balut Island in August 1993, and they kept afloat by tying together empty plastic containers. They soaked their shirts in rainwater, which they squeezed when they needed to drink. No fish dinners for them, though: they survived on decaying driftwood and by eating their own clothes!

NO BOAT for four Malaysian fishermen whose ship sank in the South China Sea in January 1997. They managed to salvage rice and biscuits, and had rainwater to drink ... but they spent 11 days adrift in two fibreglass ice-boxes before being finally picked up and taken, exhausted, to a hospital in Kuching.

ANOTHER VARIANT on the same theme: Dirk Steen, a 24-year-old German student, was rescued from Lake Michigan in July 1991. He was found floating on an air mattress 17 miles off Wilmette, Illinois, north of Chicago, and had been adrift for nearly a week. He was taken to hospital and treated for sunburn and dehydration.

POSTMAN DAVE HOCKEY, 53, crashed his Ford Orion at Shoreham, Sussex, one night in February 1995, then staggered away from the mangled car in a daze and fell into the harbour. Firemen found the wrecked car and a trail of blood, but no sign of Hockey. Then an officer shining his torch across the water saw something floating, 75 feet out to sea. At first he thought it was a buoy, but then realised that his light was actually glinting off Hockey's bald head. He had been in the water for 30 minutes by then, and when two officers swam out to his rescue he was virtually unconscious. He was treated in hospital for hypothermia and head injuries, and as one of the firemen remarked, it was only his bald pate that saved him. If he'd had a full head of hair, he wouldn't have been noticed in the dark.

A SOUTH KOREAN sailor fell overboard in the Bay of Bengal one night in 1991. Rescue came, however, in the shape of a giant turtle, and the man survived by clinging to its shell for six hours before his crew-mates found him and pulled him from the sea.

TWO YOUNG WOMEN benefited from a chain of amazing luck when they were swept off the beach at Brighton by a freak wave in September 1995. They were left clinging to the stilts of the Palace Pier with 12 foot waves breaking around them, but not long afterwards the Brighton lifeboat turned up. The lifeboat had been called out to another case, which turned out to be a hoax – but if it hadn't already been at sea, it wouldn't have reached the women in time. The story doesn't end there, though. In attempting to rescue the women, the Brighton boat crashed into the pier, and had to be rescued in turn by the lifeboat from Newhaven.

ZACHARY MAYO, 20, fell off the aircraft carrier *USS America* into the Arabian Sea in 1995. Long after all hope should have gone, he was picked up by a Pakistani trawler after treading water for a marathon 36 hours. He had used his uniform to fashion an impromptu life-saver.

18-STONE TRAWLER CAPTAIN Lance Chenery, 58, had his own in-built life-saver when he fell overboard off Queensland, Australia, in January 1989. He spent 12 hours in the sea before being picked up by a passing fishing boat, and attributed his remarkable flotation to the power of prayer... and his pot belly.

IN THE GULF OF MEXICO, Edward Shiflett, 42, had his 14-foot fishing boat capsized by the wake of a larger vessel crossing his path, in June 1986. One might think things were made worse by the fact that Shiflett had been disabled in a car crash but his wooden leg was made of balsa, and kept him afloat for two days in the shark-infested waters before he was picked up by another fisherman. "I'll never call it my bad leg again," he remarked, recovering in a Florida hospital.

LOSING A LEG ONCE might be an accident, but twice sounds like carelessness. Underwater cameraman Henry Bourse carried on filming when a shark bit off his leg and swam away with it near Melbourne. The lost leg, fortunately, was artificial but it was a replacement for his real leg, which had been bitten off by another shark in a similar attack several years earlier.

THREE CHILDREN playing on the beach at Newton Point, Porthcawl, in Wales, were suddenly swept out to sea by a huge wave in August 1992. But, just as suddenly, they were swept straight back again by another wave, and deposited safely on the beach.

LOBSTERMAN Geoff Barth was flung out of his boat in September 1993 by huge waves when the engine failed and, weighed down by heavy boots and clothes, was being carried away from the shore of Newport, Rhode Island. Help was at hand, however, in the shape of angler Ray Smith, who cast his line and 80 feet offshore, Barth managed to catch it. Amazingly, the line held as Smith slowly reeled in Barth, weighing 150 lb, and safely landed his catch. Smith added: "I may try for a wind surfer next time — more challenging."

ANOTHER FISHY TALE: Hank Vandorn, 50, and his son Henry, 17, were cut off by the rising tide on a sandbank in the Bristol Channel in April 1997. They jammed their fishing rods into the sand, and then used them as stilts as the water rose around them. Hank also blew up a bin-liner to act as a float, and they hung on for two hours before being rescued.

THREE MEN were cruising on the Hudson River in New York state in 1986, when a storm blew up and washed both them and their boat ashore, straight onto an adjacent railway line. Shortly afterwards, the boat was struck by a northbound train. The crew escaped with their lives; the boat was destroyed; the train was late.

POSTMAN COLIN CHASE, 20, was on holiday in Majorca in 1977, and was wading along the coast through shallow water. He couldn't swim, but as the water only came up to his waist and there were people standing up in the sea at least 60 yards further out, there seemed nothing to worry about. Then he stepped into a huge hole in the seabed and plunged below the water. He was well on the way to drowning when a German skindiver swam by, pulled him out of the sea, and gave him artificial respiration. Even more fortunately, just at that moment an ambulance drove by. Chase came to on the way to hospital, where he was kept for five days and treated for the effects of swallowing sea water. Returning home to Clapham, he vowed that the first thing he was going to do was learn to swim.

FAR IN THE NORTH, Henrik Carlsen, 30, set off from his Upernavik home in Greenland in his boat, ready for a day's fishing, in October 1992. But the boat got caught in pack-ice, and he was stranded on deserted Nunarssuaq Island. He was wearing dungarees, a shirt, a thin jacket and trainers, had no flares or food, and the wind was dropping the temperature to minus 30 degrees farenheit. Overturning his dinghy on the beach, he crawled inside and ate snow to survive.

A five-day search by planes and helicopters failed to find him. After 15 days, though, two Inuit passed by in their kayak and saw an old rowing boat that Carlsen had raised upright to draw attention. They alerted Greenland police, who found Carlsen, frostbitten in both feet and three stone lighter for his ordeal... but alive.

IT'S NOT THE SORT OF THING you expect when you decide to go for a quick swim at a beach party, but Ron Bakx suddenly found himself attacked by a six-foot crocodile in November 1997, after he dived into the sea off Yorkeys Knob, near Cairns in Queensland. The water was only waist deep, but the croc soon had Bakx's head and shoulder in its jaws, and was trying to roll and drag him under. Bakx, 35, hit back in the only way he could – with his fists. The beast eventually let go, and he ran back to shore, to be taken to hospital for treatment to cuts on his head, arm, back and right shoulder. And in case you're wondering what his friends were doing all the time he was in the water yelling and fighting... yes, they stayed right where they were on the beach and watched.

GOLDEN GAMBLES
AND RUNS OF LUCK

Some folks just can't stop winning and some just can't
stop escaping. These will run and run...

POOR FARMER Hüdai Onur, 33, was a father of two from
Isabey village in Turkey, but he obviously liked to play the lotteries. On 1 October 1991 he won 20 million lira (£2,200) on
Spur-Loto. A month later, on 1 November, he won 980 million
lira (£109,000) from Spor-Toto. Then on 19 January 1992 he
won 2,500 million lira (£280,000) from the national lottery,
Milli Piyango. By this time he had won all the main legal lotteries in Turkey, and then, on 27 January, his father-in-law
died and left him a large field and vineyard besides.

CALIFORNIAN AUTHOR and golfer Scott Palmer, 26, hit a
hole-in-one 18 times between June 1983 and the following
January, his drives having hit the pin on 50 other occasions
besides. And he collected affidavits from 65 witnesses to prove

it, too. *Golf Digest* somehow calculated the odds on hitting a hole (once) from the tee at 33,616 to one. Four of his holes-in-one came on consecutive days; seven of them were on par-4 holes and the average length for all 18 was 209 yards. At the instant he made the charmed strokes, he would, for some reason, get a mental image of a faceless woman pouring a glass of milk. And as if all this wasn't bad enough, halfway through his lucky streak, he first started talking golf lessons!

A CHARMED LIFE had Pedro Gaitan Puentes of Colombia, though his offspring weren't so lucky. He survived when a plane crashed in rain and fog near a national park 100 miles south-west of Bogota, in September 1995. All four crew and 16 passengers were killed, including his nine-year-old son Camilo, but Pedro escaped with cuts and bruises. As he lay in hospital, his strange tale emerged: only a month before he had survived a bus accident on a mountain road, without injury. And seven years before that, he had left the town of Armero, in central Colombia, the day before a volcano erupted and buried the town. Nearly all the 23,000 inhabitants were killed, including his daughter. Pedro came out a triple winner... but with his other losses, maybe he didn't consider himself so lucky after all.

JOSEPH CROWLEY, sharing a surname with a certain magician called Aleister who claimed to be the Great Beast 666, had wizard luck in 1993 when he won £2 million in the Ohio Lottery. The retired construction worker from Boca Raton then proceeded to scoop a £13 million jackpot in the Florida Lotto. The 66-year old was due to be paid 20 annual payments of $1 million (£666,000).

THE RUN WAS THERE, but the luck wasn't. Barbara Newell obviously had the odds on her side in an Adelaide casino when she threw 21 consecutive tails in a two-up ring, which is a four million to one occurrence. Unfortunately she only won $262.50 instead of a fortune, because she didn't change her original bet.

PUB MANAGER Richard Connolly, from Douglas, Isle of Man, went to the Palace Casino on the night of his 23rd birthday. That fell on 23 September 1992, so at 23:23 that evening he placed a bet of £23 on the roulette wheel's number 23, and won £571. "I was staggered when the ball popped into 23," he said, but he should really have had the courage of his convictions. If he'd resisted the temptation to hedge the bet by splitting it between the numbers on each side, he would have won far more.

IT WAS THE HOUSE which had the luck at the Stakis Club in Bristol, where croupier Liz Harlow-Smith was operating the roulette wheel. The number four came up a record seven times in a row, at odds, we're told, of almost 100 billion to one. But no one had chosen to bet on the number. Had a punter put £10 on four and let his winnings ride, he would have ended up with £949 billion. The previous roulette record was set in Puerto Rico in 1959, when the same number came up six times running.

AN AUSTRIAN TEACHER planned to lose £20 on a fruit-machine in Graz to demonstrate the evils of gambling to his pupils... but instead he won £150,000. His name was Helfried Luck.

A STREET VENDOR cleaning a fish in the Caribbean port of Turbo found what looked like the number 1124 on its side. As a result, about 300 people were inspired to use the number in the Colombian lottery and won over a million pounds.

THE SAME THING happened again in January 1999, although this time the numbered beast was a frog. Liliana Artega found it in her garden in San Juan de Acosta and noticed some purplish markings on one leg, which her son Carlos interpreted as the numbers 8794. The Artegas used the numbers in the local lottery and won £50,000. This was apparently the second lottery-winning numbered frog in the town within six months, sending the population into a frenzy of frog-hunting.

SOME PEOPLE will bet on anything, regardless of taste or discretion, and quite a lot of them seem to be in Connecticut. On 20 July 1996, only a week after the jumbo jet, TWA 800, crashed into the Atlantic with the loss of all aboard, 6,208 people put their money on 8-0-0 in the state's daily lottery. The number came up and the state had to pay out just over $1 million, about three times what was wagered.

A GOLDEN HANDSHAKE for office worker Frederick Baum when he was made redundant in Munich in 1995. While clearing out his desk, he found a blank football pools coupon, filled it in and mailed it off. He won £400,000.

THE NAME Banks is the most common, as well as the most appropriate, name among winners of Littlewood's Lotteries scratchcards, beating off the more obviously common names like Smith, Jones and Brown. And it won't be a surprise to hear that in Bordeaux, south-west France, the winners of a £1 million pound lottery prize were M. and Mme Lotterie.

LOTTERIES ARE AN OBSESSION in the Orient, and Thailand is no exception. Luang Phor Khoon, the country's most popular Buddhist monk, has gained a wide following because people believe that if he hits them on the head with a rolled-up newspaper, they have a better chance of winning the state lottery. One can only wonder how this notion got started in the first place.

ALSO IN THAILAND, another monk stole the eggs of two boa constrictors in April 1998, claiming that he could predict the winning lottery numbers from them. Whether he could or not – or how he could – remains unknown, as the police intervened and made him give them back.

BULGARIAN ROCK CLIMBER Ivan Dobromi really pushed his luck on Mont Blanc in 1990. First he fell 20 feet down a cliff and hurt his back. Deciding it wasn't too serious, he carried on, but got lost in a storm and miraculously managed to miss dozens of deep crevasses. Later, hundreds of feet up an ice face, he dropped his climbing hooks and was left clinging to an ice pick. A rescue helicopter was sent out to pick him up, but when he waved at the pilot, he let go of the ice pick and fell 600 feet. He landed in a snow drift only inches from another cliff, and survived the whole ordeal with little more than bruises.

ANOTHER RUN of lucky escapes for John Doyle, 12, who was on his first trainspotting trip in July 1984, at Bradwell in Buckinghamshire. He fell off a 20-foot high bridge over the main line from Euston to the Midlands and hit 25,000 volt power cables, causing an explosion, then plunged onto concrete and iron rails below. Then he was dragged clear by his friends just before an Inter-City train roared over the track. Meanwhile, a huge undergrowth fire had been started by the power-cable explosion, but that spread away from him. Trains were halted for three hours while firemen rescued the boy and fought the blaze. He had taken the full force of the electricity through his body, and left a burn-mark on the bridge in the shape of a hand where he touched it on the way down, but he escaped with only a burn on his ankle.

GOD TOLD HER to do it, it seems, and Jeffie Harvey, 32, of Chicago, followed orders to the letter in 1981. She had lost her money on the way to the supermarket to buy milk and nappies for her baby, but going through her pockets she managed to find one last dollar. Then a voice told her to buy a lottery ticket on the Illinois State Lottery with it. That ticket gave her the winning horse in the Arlington Million race – and Jeffie, in turn, won a million dollars too.

EVERYTHING LOOKED ROSY for an unnamed 52-year-old man from Toulouse when he won £286,000 on the national lottery, but he managed to fritter it all away, and ended up facing bankruptcy. His telephone had been cut off, his car repossessed, and his family were facing expulsion from their home. Then, just when the bailiffs were closing in, in July 1992, he won the lottery again! This time it was £1,800,000, which presumably would have taken him a little longer to spend!

BRIDE-TO-BE Jeanette Towle, 22, had arranged a honeymoon holiday to Jamaica in June 1992, and was just about to pay for it... when she won exactly the same trip in a contest at Gedling, Notts.

PUNTER FRANK THOROUGHGOOD'S number was almost up in June 1991. The 85-year-old retired groundsman was in such a hurry to collect his winning bet that he decided to take a short-cut to the bookies, and fell into a swamp at Ferndown, Bournemouth. And there he stayed through a cold night, stuck in mud that came up to his chest, until a passing motorist spotted him waving his walking stick late the following morning. He was finally rescued after 19 hours, when a dozen firemen inched along extension ladders to reach him. Was it worth it? Frank was collecting on a 40p forecast on the greyhounds... that won him the princely sum of £3.20.

ONE OF THE GREAT escapers was Harry Shaw, and his run of luck began at just 14 years old, when he survived a 60 foot fall. In later years, he was hit by a car and dragged underneath it, then came World War II, where he survived shells and machine-gun bullets at Dunkirk, and was the sole survivor of a bombed hospital ward. After that he was in a van that over-turned, and was also knocked down by a van in another accident. But the retired postman from Darley Abbey, Derby, took it all in his stride... and eventually died peacefully in his bed in December 1986, at the age of 83.

CHAPTER FIFTEEN

WEATHER OR NOT

Hurricanes, tornadoes, storms and floods...
sometimes we escape them all.

A PEASANT WOMAN called Yang Youxiang, 40, was caught in a storm at Liaoqiao township in China's Hubei province in May 1985. Fortunately, she had her umbrella with her as she walked home through the fields, but unfortunately a tornado then struck. Hanging on grimly to the treasured brolly, she was lifted high into the air, and then deposited 550 yards away on the far side of the Jiuda river. After treatment for hailstone injuries, she returned to work.

UP TO TEN TORNADOES cut a swathe across Florida in February 1998, killing 38 people and injuring more than 250. Jonathan Waldick, an 18-month-old toddler, was asleep in his parents' wood-framed house in Kissimmee when one of the tornados struck. As rain and hail pelted down, the 260 mph wind destroyed the house. Jonathan's great-grandmother,

Shirley Driver, awoke to find his four-year-old sister Destiny safe beside her, but the toddler was nowhere in sight. He was only found after a 45 minute search, and he was still in bed. The twister had carried Jonathan and his mattress outside, snapped the top off a large oak tree, and then deposited both boy and mattress in the branches. His only injury was a small bump on the head.

IN CHINA, a much more alarming freak wind struck in 1986, roaring through the western oasis of Hami. This one sucked 13 schoolchildren into the air and carried them for 12 miles, before putting them down unharmed in sand dunes and scrub. The children were eventually found two days later, suffering only from scratches caused by the swirling sands.

IT ISN'T JUST PEOPLE who get carried off by winds, of course. Sam the cat got just as lucky in August 1998. A tornado flattened the house of his owners, Paul and Chris Staten, in Greenfield, Indiana, and a frantic search of the debris produced no sign of Sam. Four days later, a friend called to say that the flying cat had been found, injured, at a neighbour's house, also in the tornado's path, four miles away.

MOST PARACHUTISTS head down toward the ground, but Didier Dahran, 27, went the other way – up! It all started well enough, when Dahran made a training jump at Bouloc, southwest France, in May 1993. Falling to 1,000 feet and preparing for a routine landing, he suddenly found himself sucked into a freak cyclonic current, and shot up even faster than he'd been coming down. Helpless and terrified, he watched the reading on his wrist altimeter soar to 25,000 feet, before it jammed at its maximum. Soaked by rain, blinded by cloud and struggling to breathe in the thin air, he found himself in temperatures of minus 30 degrees centigrade, and his face and hands froze. Eventually, after two hours in which he was close to losing consciousness, his regular parachute collapsed and he started plummetting toward the ground. He just managed to launch his emergency chute before passing out completely, and landed heavily, by twilight, 30 miles from where he had started out. He had no broken bones or major injuries, though he was hospitalised for severe frostbite and shock.

GARY SEAGRAVE, 51, had gone to Laguna Beach, Florida, to pick up his daughter who had been stranded by mudslides and tornadoes in February 1998. Some strangers offered him a bed for the night, but another mudslide swept him out of the house. When he stopped rolling, he ended up on a pile of rocks, twigs and living-room furniture, next to a cat shelter. Though he'd lost his glasses, he noticed that there was baby lying next to him, still alive.

Nine-month old Tiffany Sarabia had ridden the wave of mud that swept her from her cot and out into the night. Seagrave handed the girl to a passerby, who rushed her to paramedics who, in turn, put her in an ambulance. Meanwhile, Tiffany's barely-conscious mother, Teresa, had been loaded into the same ambulance. Immediately on waking, she screamed for her baby, only to find her unharmed on the adjoining stretcher. The mudslide had killed two men and destroyed two houses.

AN UNEXPLAINED CHANGE of sleeping position saved 18-month-old Joshua Mello when a hurricane hit Paxton, Massachusetts, in August 1976. The hurricane brought down a tree, which crashed through the roof of his parents' caravan, then smashed the end of the infant's crib. Joshua had always slept with his head at that end of the crib... but this particular night he turned around, and the tree missed his legs by an inch.

HER PARENTS didn't like it, but Hayley Chidgey, 15, had the belly-ring put in anyway. Two weeks later, as she walked home in Harefield, Middlesex, in September 1997, she was struck by two lightning bolts, and her passion for body-piercing saved her life. Doctors at the Royal London Hospital told her that she survived because the jewellery diverted the electric charge, and stopped it travelling through her inside her chest.

AN ENGLISHMAN, as we know, should never be without his brolly. But sometimes it does more than just keep the rain off. Patrick Leyden was using his umbrella for the usual purpose in 1989, as he walked through Newcastle-under-Lyme, Staffs when the rain turned a mite unusual: a window-frame fell on him from the upper storey of a shop. It bounced off the brolly, and he escaped unhurt.

AND OTHERS ...

Dame Fortune is fickle... and sometimes she doesn't seem to know what's she's up to! A miscellany of extraordinary escapes and uncategorizable accidents.

A FALLEN ANGEL nearly finished off Ken Seymour, 52, in December 1991. He was shopping in Plymouth city centre when the four-foot illuminated angel fell from an overhead display and crashed at his feet. "It wasn't a guardian angel," he remarked.

HILTON MARTIN, 41, was cleaning his lavatory in Satellite Beach, near Cape Canaveral, Florida, in September 1985. He used Comet brand cleanser in the cistern tank, and hung a Sani-Flush block inside. As the water started bubbling, the telephone rang. He rushed to answer it, though it stopped before he could pick up the receiver. Just as well, because then he heard a noise behind him "like a hand grenade going off". An explosion had blown the special-order lavatory and tank to pieces. Fire officials were stumped, but it was suggested that the calcium hypochloride in Sani-Flush could have explosively combined with the hydrocarbons in the Comet. Spokespeople for both companies denied this was possible, but that seems to avoid the main question: who phoned at just the right time?

A MOROCCAN hashish dealer was transporting his wares with a donkey in 1993, when he was arrested near the town of Al-Hoceima. As the police waited for a car to take the man to prison, the donkey ate the drugs and the man was released for lack of evidence. The donkey was later found in a coma. Wonder if he had a good time before he passed out?

SMOKE ALARMS always seem like a good idea, and in 1993 Bob Jones, 27, fixed one to the ceiling of his basement flat in Halifax, Yorkshire, with sticky tape. Eventually the battery ran down and the alarm began to bleep a warning, so Bob removed the battery... and then forgot to replace it. A few days later he fell asleep after some friends had been to visit. A fire broke out, believed to have been caused by a lighted cigarette slipping between the cushions of an armchair. Bob slept on, until the flames reached the ceiling and melted the tape, at which point the inoperative smoke alarm fell squarely on Bob's head. He woke to choking smoke and escaped the flames just in time, though he still had to be treated in hospital for smoke inhalation.

NO ONE SEEMS TO KNOW quite why he did it, but in May 1995 two-year-old Kolby Grinston decided to set off the fire alarm at the Kiddie Kove Nursery in Chicago. Then he marched outside with his classmates, just as they had been trained to do. Moments later a car ran through a red light and struck a second car, which smashed into the nursery as the children stood outside. The car ploughed through a play kitchen and came to a halt on top of some lockers used by the youngsters. The school's director, Olivia Hargon, said that if Kolby hadn't pulled the alarm, the children would have been at the lockers putting their jackets away. But despite the obvious escape from major fatalities, the story didn't end quite as happily as it should. Somehow a van, hit by the second car, bumped into the children as they were going back into school, and 14 of them, between four and six, were slightly injured.

WENDY SEAL of Derby was vacuuming the floor in 1996, when her 11-month-old daughter Lauren bit clean through the electric flex. Wendy immediately pulled out the plug, but was convinced her daughter had died – smoke was coming out of the sides of her mouth and her hair was standing on end. Nonetheless, Lauren was rushed to hospital, and a few hours later she was gurgling happily, in perfect health apart from a slight blister on her mouth.

SOME MIGHT THINK it a good way to go, but in May 1990 Ian Button, 23, was almost undone when a 25,000 litre vat of red wine exploded at the vineyard where he worked in Lamberhurst, Kent. He ran for his life, but within seconds the tide of wine was five feet deep, surging round his neck ... but then just as suddenly the level dropped as the wine surged on to flood offices and a courtyard outside. Soaked and reeking of drink, Button escaped unscathed.

A FIRE broke out in a bathroom extractor fan at Jeff Crooks' house in Wolverhampton in November 1995. Heat from the fire burned through the fan's plastic surround and the motor fell out, hitting an ærosol can of shaving cream. The can exploded, spraying foam everywhere and putting the fire out. Or so it seemed to Crooks... he couldn't say for sure, as he'd slept right through the crisis.

ANOTHER BATHROOM FIRE was swiftly put out in Armthorpe, Yorkshire, in October 1991. The unnamed family living in the house were out for the day, but had left a heater on which set fire to the bathroom curtains. These then fell down and set the carpet alight, but the fire melted the plastic toilet cistern, which dumped a full tank of water on the floor and extinguished the flames. Even more astonishingly, melted plastic sealed the cistern, preventing further flooding. The family reurned to find little more than smoke damage.

COLIN GELL accidentally stuck a crowbar through an 11,000 volt cable at Quorn, Leicestershire, but simply stood there with a tingling in one arm as sparks showered round him. He was wearing rubber wellington boots, which saved his life – but nearby 500 homes were blacked out.

A TRAMP decided to spend the night in a giant rubbish bin at a shopping centre in Kettering, Northants, in April 1981. Bad choice. As he was still sleeping when the bin was about to be tipped into the local council's refuse crushing machine the following morning. He only escaped mangling when one of the dustmen noticed his arm sticking out of the rubbish, but after being dragged from his bed the tramp left without saying a word. We have several similar tales of "escape from the crushing machine" which suggests that this thing happens rather often (and for every one who escaped, how many didn't?). Or perhaps this has become another urban legend...

A DIFFERENT TWIST for homeless tramp Andy Orton, 53, of Chicago, Illinois. In February 1995, he was sleeping on the top floor of a derelict building when a demolition crew blew it up. "I was taking a nap on the top floor," he said, "when suddenly everything went black and I was on the ground floor in a pile of rubble." He escaped without a scratch, though, and was released after a night's observation in hospital.

IT ALWAYS PAYS to kiss the wife goodbye, as Roderick Long, 33, discovered in February 1981. She was driving him to work that night in Pittsfield, Pennsylvania, but stopped at a 50-foot bridge which had been damaged by ice earlier in the day. Long didn't want them to drive across it, and decided to walk instead, but shortly after he started off he paused and turned round, because he'd forgotten that goodbye kiss. Just then, the 25-foot centre section of the bridge fell into the swollen creek beneath. Long would otherwise have been carried away by the waters, probably to his death.

STAYING AT HOME usually seems like a safe option, but Norma Pinchin and her disabled husband John found that wasn't quite the case in December 1992. They were minding their own business happily in Watchfield, Wilts, when an ærial fell off a jumbo jet passing overheard, plunged straight through the roof, and scythed into a basket of washing at Norma's feet.

SUDDENLY CONFRONTED by an oncoming train in November 1979 as he stood on a level-crossing at Vimmerby, Sweden, an 82-year-old man promptly fainted. That saved his life, as he fell between the tracks, and the train passed over without hitting him.

MOST FOLKS use cameras for taking pictures with, but an unnamed Italian hiker used his as a life-saver in January 1998. He was walking on the flank of Monte Generosso, in the Swiss Alps, when he fell 400 metres down a steep slope and injured his ribs. After dark, he used the flash of his disposable camera to make light signals which could be seen several kilometres away, and a mountain rescue team was sent to find him. They saved him from freezing overnight, and he was taken to hospital by helicopter the following morning.

A BEDTIME DRINK of cocoa was suddenly interrupted, in April 1994, as 80-year-old Giuseppina Tagliabue was sitting on her fold-up bed in Milan. With rather inappropriate timing, the bed did just what it was supposed to do and suddenly snapped shut, trapping the old lady for two days. Eventually her son Mario broke into the flat after he failed to contact her, describing the scene as seeming "like a huge sandwich with mother as the meat in the middle." He managed to release her unharmed, though.

A NARROW SQUEAK for reservist Michael Trout, 21, called up to fight in the Gulf War of 1991. Trout, from Greensburg, Pennsylvania, was playing Trivial Pursuit with eight other soldiers at Dharhan, Saudi Arabia, when he spotted a mouse. Perhaps surprisingly for a soldier, Trout was scared of mice, so he left the group... moments before a Scud missile hit the barracks. Six of his comrades were killed, but Trout had moved far enough away to survive with ear damage and shrapnel wounds.

FIVE PEOPLE were killed when two trains collided head-on in Mexico in February 1991. Casualties could have been much worse though, but for the fact that one train was carrying two freight cars full of toilet paper, which absorbed some of the impact. So that's what they mean about "absorbent tissue."

FORGETFULNESS isn't usually a good thing, but it saved Peter Ewing's life in November 1989. He was heading for his car, in Upper Westwood, Wilts, when he suddenly remembered that he'd forgotten a file. As he turned round to collect it from his desk, a five ton crane fell on his car and flattened it.

GOING THROUGH her safety deposit box one Saturday in August 1994, Pushpa Singhiana, 52, was suddenly plunged into darkness when the lights went out and the vault door closed. She was stuck in the Calcutta vault for three days, and survived by chanting religious verses and swallowing her own saliva. A cleaner finally heard her voice when he started work on the following Tuesday morning.

That wasn't the end of the story, though. Bank officials, in full view of the police, refused to open the vault until the Singhiana family promised in writing not to sue the bank for negligence. The door was only opened after the family threatened to break it open themselves.

THE EMERGENCY SWITCHBOARD OPERATOR was, understandably, sceptical when he received a call from a man on a mobile phone saying that he was hanging off a cliff by his fingernails. "How have you dialled this number?" he asked. "I pressed the re-dial button with my nose!" screamed Christian Raymond before bursting into tears, which finally convinced the operator that he was telling the truth.

Raymond, a 23-year-old shepherd, was 2,000 metres up in the Dent de Crolles region of the French Chartreuse mountains when he slipped down a slope, in October 1998. While trying to cling on to tufts of grass, he managed to get his mobile phone out of his bag, but no sooner had he got through to the emergency operator for the first time, than the connection failed. After that, he lost his grip and slid further, toward a deep ravine but the phone slipped down the slope after him and, miraculously, ended up near his face ... close enough for the nasal re-dial. He was eventually rescued by helicopter 17 minutes later. A case which gives a whole new meaning to "hanging on the phone"!

NOT QUITE what we usually mean by a "lucky escape" but a giant lizard wandered into a courtroom in Mombasa, Kenya, in October 1995, and caused a general stampede. In the panic, 20 prisoners slipped away from their warders and made for freedom.

WHEN STEVE WALTERS tugged some concrete from the ground while fixing a garden fence at his home in Kitt's Green, Birmingham, in March 1997, he suddenly found the ground giving way beneath him. A previously-hidden Victorian well, 40 feet deep, had opened up, and the 36-year-old metal worker fell straight into it... or rather he didn't fall, because his 56-inch beer-belly got stuck in the mouth of the well. And there he stayed, listening to the rubble crashing into the well beneath him, for 15 minutes, until his wife and neighbours managed to pull him out. It turned out afterwards that there was 10 feet of water at the bottom of the well, and Walters couldn't swim either; so if the fall hadn't killed him he would probably have drowned. Walters drank 100 pints of beer a week and wasn't intending to stop – if he'd taken his doctor's advice and dieted, he'd probably be dead.

DISOBEDIENT CHILDREN are a mother's despair, but sometimes it's good to be bad. Simon Cooley, 12, came home from football practice in January 1976, and his mother told him to go upstairs and change. Instead, he opted to watch television in the sitting room... and so escaped when the chimney fell through the ceiling of his bedroom at the mediæval Sun Hotel, in Brill, Bucks.

FLYING CARPETS are one thing... but it was a flying mattress that saved the life of 79-year-old James Steuer of Crystal Lake, Illinois. Steuer was sitting on his bed one morning in January 1989, putting on his shoes in preparation for a visit to his daughter-in-law, when a sudden explosion levelled his house. Moments later, Steuer was still sitting on the mattress, but it was outside in the driveway, blown through a side wall of the house by the blast. The gas explosion scattered broken glass everywhere, threw a side wall against his neighbour's garage, sent pieces of wood onto neighbours' rooftops and gave off such a blast of heat that it melted the side-cladding of a neighbouring house. It also burned down Steuer's house, of course, and set fire to the mattress he'd ridden on as well. Steuer escaped with minor scratches ... but he did have a request for the firefighters who came to his assistance: "Do you think you could find my car keys and glasses?"

IF THERE'S ONE THING you don't expect to do in a lift, it's drown. But businessman Jacques Dehaes, of Lille, France, got into the lift at his apartment block in July 1981, pressed the button that should have taken him from the ground to the fourth floor – and plunged instead into the basement, which had been flooded after a recent cloudburst. Within two minutes, the lift was flooded and Dehaes, 40, found himself frantically doing the breaststroke to keep afloat. Fortunately, the water stopped rising three inches from the lift roof, giving him enough air to breathe, and he was eventually rescued by firemen.

A DIET of spaghetti hoops isn't usually considered a life-saver, but that was the favourite food, it seems, of Danish Vice Consul Klaus Bogstad and his family. When fire broke out in the kitchen of their house in Ham, Surrey, one night in November 1980, the sound of exploding spaghetti cans woke

Bogstad's wife Sheila, and the couple and their two sons fled the burning building down a fire-escape.

BAD ENOUGH, one might think, to be bitten by a Western Brown snake, one of Australia's deadliest, on its own – or to be attacked by the similarly deadly Red Back spider, on its own. Carol Mathews, however, managed to get bitten by both at once in March 1994. The 42-year-old was in a storeroom in a supermarket she runs in Alice Springs when she felt a pin-prick on each leg. Looking down, she saw the snake suspended in the web of the spider, and both of them struck out at her together. She was rushed to Alice Springs Hospital and given anti-venom, saying later that the only effect from the attacks was a bad headache.

A HOAX CALL to the fire brigade actually helped save an old woman's life in a real fire in August 1979. The firemen were just round the corner at the site of the hoax call, in Liverpool, when the real emergency message came through, and reached the actual fire in only two minutes instead of the usual four or five. There they found smoke belching from the window of a first-floor flat, and within was pensioner Elsie Audley, lying unconscious on the floor. Using breathing apparatus, the fire-men broke in and dragged her clear, giving her oxygen until the ambulance arrived. She recovered in hospital from the effects of smoke-inhalation.

PERHAPS THE MOST FAMOUS of narrow escapes was that of John Lee, sentenced to death for murdering his employer, an elderly widow, in 1885. He was taken to the gallows in Exeter Prison, the trap was tested, the noose was placed round his neck. But the trap failed to open underneath him... not once, or twice, but three times, in spite of the hangman stamping on it. The prison governor was so impressed that the execution was cancelled, and his sentence was eventually commuted to life imprisonment. Lee became known as "the man they couldn't hang," served 30 years in prison, and then emigrated to America and married.

REFERENCES

UP IN THE AIR

Plane of priests: *Guardian*, 3 Dec 1993. Fall into snow drift: *D.Mail*, 4 Nov 1997. Colombian air-crash: *D.Mail*, 13 Jan 1995, etc. Self-landing plane: *Spokane Spokesman Review*, 13 Dec 1997. Russian transport: *International Combat Arms*, May 1989. Wheel-well stowaway: *[AP]*, 6 June 1993. Soft cheese: *S.Express*, 3 Dec 1995. Radioing pilot: *The European*, 17 Dec 1992. Wobbly Boeing: *Washington Post*, 25 July 1997. Premature ejection: *D.Telegraph*, 4 April 1994. Sky-diver/plane crash: *NY Daily News*, 27 Nov 1993; *D.Mirror*, 8 Oct 1996. Hang-glider: *D.Mirror*, 8 April 1993. Aeroflot lemonade: *[AP]*, 8 May 1994. Hydraulic urination: *North Tahoe Truckee Week*, 9 June 1994. Tail-sitter: *South China Morning Post*, 17 April 1992. Sucked through window: *D.Telegraph*, 11 June 1990. Dog-bite: *Mail on Sunday*, 27 Sept 1992. Near-missile: *Tampa Tribune*, 27 June 1987.

BITING THE BULLET

Post office: *D.Mirror*, 19 March 1993. Nightclub boss: *D.Mirror*, 25 March 1992. Mormon: *D.Telegraph*, 3 June 1998. False teeth: *[AP]*, 14 June, 1992. Christ statuette: *Sun*, 24 June 1998. Detouring bullets: *Sun*, 15 Oct 1974 + 20 Jan 1975. Spectacles: *National Enquirer*, 26 Aug 1975. Wallet: *[AP]*, 1 Feb 1992. Credit-cards: *People*, 18 April 1993. Tie knot: *International Herald Tribune*, 9 Dec 1991. Chequebook: *Cleveland Plain Dealer*, 26 March 1992. Back tooth: *[AP]*, 17 Sept 1990. Bullet in gun barrel: *Indianapolis Star*, 23 Oct 1987. Prayer book: *D.Telegraph*, 9 Feb 1990. Zipper: *Harrisburg Sunday Patriot News*, 14 Jan 1990. Spoon: *Victoria Times-Colonist*, 1 March 1993. Door key: *Belfast Telegraph*, 2 April 1993. Mobile phone: *[R]*, 15 June 1993. Breast implant: *People*, 17 Oct 1993. Amulet: *Guardian*, 8 April 1993, etc. Rabbit: *The News (Portsmouth)*, 26 Oct 1993. Lottery tickets: *[AP]*, 29 April 1997. Coins: *[R]*, 1 May 1997. Penny pick-up: *D.Mirror*, 5 Oct 1982. Mints: *D.Mail*, 26 Feb 1997. Bullet-proof vest: *News of the World*, 11 Dec 1977. Nose-blown bullet:

Washington Post, 25 Dec 1992. Gold necklace: *[AP]*, 25 May 1993. Garfield: *Columbia Dispatch*, 20 Sept 1989. Pinochet: *Independent*, 1 Oct 1988. Sandwich: *NY Post*, 27 March 1994. Pen: *[AP]*, 5 June 1996.

IT WAS JUST THERE...

Bamboo thicket: *Independent*, 17 April 1989. Safe full of money: *Middlesbrough Evening Gazette*, 30 June 1989. Diamond pasta: *D.Mirror*, 26 April, 1996. Rainbow ring: *Guardian*, 5 Oct 1989. Scorpion chasers: *[AFP]*, 14 April 1994. Diamond doll: *Weekly News*, 27 July 1996. Yam diamond: *[R]*, 29 Jan 1997. Tucson bills: *[AP]*, 20 Jan 1999. Note in shark: *Weekly News*, 22 Feb 1975.

HORRORS!

Chainsaw: *Houston Chronicle*, 4 Aug 1984. Power-saw: *St Louis Sun*, 10 Dec 1984. Well: *[AP]*, 13 Oct 1997. Road roller: *Times*, 22 Jan 1998, etc. Sleepwalker: *[AP]*, 26 Nov 1998. Irishman: *D.Express*, 18 Aug 1979. Abandoned baby: *D.Mirror*, 15 Oct 1990. Nail in heart: *Europa Times*, ? Dec 1993. Nail in head: *S.Express*, 18 Nov 1979. Rod impalement: *San José Mercury News*, 30 Nov 1988. Chest stake: *Sun*, 25 April 1985. Skull crowbar: *[AP]*, 5 May + 28 July 1981. Mincing machine: *D.Star*, 21 April 1994. Neck knife: *Eve. Standard (London)*, 10 Feb 1997.

ON THE ROAD

Kim Won-Sun: *Sun*, 6 May 1989. Landing strip: *[AP]*, 8 Aug 1997. Cyclist: *[AP]*, 19 May 1998. Extinguisher van: *D.Telegraph*, 6 June 1998. Coin in throat: *D.Telegraph*, 9 June 1998. Skewered car: *Western Morning News*, 20 August 1998. Ayers Rock: *D.Mail*, 9 July 1998. Plummetting Volvo:

Independent, 13 Jan 1996. Blazing Renault: *News of the World*, 28 Jan 1999. Cliff Skoda: *Wolverhampton Express & Star*, 28 April 1994. Baby on roof: *Hartford Courant*, 16 Oct 1995. Nissan cliff-fall: *D.Telegraph*, 30 Aug 1994. Scaffolding: *D.Mirror*, 8 Oct 1997. Tanker: *D.Mirror*, 21 March 1974. Steel: *D.Record*, 4 March 1995. Car under lorry: *Western Morning News*, 5 Jan 1993. Cliff couch: *Cleveland Plain Dealer*, 15 March 1986. Wheel through window: *Sun*, 1 May 1992. Fat Frenchman: *D.Star*, 9 May 1992. Smoke-cloud: *Gloucestershire Echo*, 8 Oct 1992. Apples: *Coventry Evening Telegraph*, 16 Jan 1998. Dead phone: *D.Star*, 10 July 1991.

SAVED BY THE...

Macaw: *D.Telegraph*, 19 Feb 1998. Pele: *Nairobi Standard*, 7 Jan 1991. Wrong number: *Houston Chronicle*, 2 Nov 1985. Whale: *Canberra Times*, 21 Sept 1985. Lobster rescue: *Times*, 20 July 1994. Batman: *D.Mirror*, 14 Nov 1987. Sleep rescue: *S.Telegraph*, 7 Aug 1994. Bagpipe music: *Dallas Morning News*, 16 June 1997. Minefield ghost: *D.Mail*, 22 Nov 1997. Wheat-planter: *Atlanta Constitution*, 8 Oct 1990. Japanese drunk: *[R]*, 2 March 1993.

A BUNCH OF BOOMERANGS

Caterpillar brooch: *Nottingham Evening Post*, 24 July 1997. Beach ring: *D.Mirror*, 19 July 1979. Ring in coral: *Philadelphia Daily News*, 4 Feb 1999. Ring in carrot: *Sydsvenska Dagbladet*, 18 Aug 1996. Ring in chicken: *Sun*, 6 Feb 1975. Earring in pub: *Times*, 6 Feb 1999. Cap & pipe: *D.Telegraph*, 22 March 1975. Licence in fish: *St Catherines Standard*, 10 Sept 1983. Watch in pike: *D.Telegraph*, 16 Aug 1979. Sea spectacles: *S.Express*, 13 Nov 1971. Book: *Sun*, 22 June 1980. Medal: *S.Express*, 7 Oct 1979. Tramp's money: *St Louis Post-Despatch*, 2 Nov 1985. Falcon: *Derby Evening Telegraph*, 10 Feb 1995. Yaska: *Eve. Standard (London)*, 23 July

1997. Nightclub watch: *Newcastle Journal*, 1 Nov 1996. Camera: *Times*, 27 Aug 1997.

BACK FROM THE DEAD

Badawi: *Manchester Evening News*, 14 July 1997. Troche: *[AP]*, 4 Feb 1985. Kostichka: *S.Telegraph (S. Australia)*, 3 March 1985. Tontlewicz: *Omaha World Herald*, 22 Jan 1984; *International Herald Tribune*, 16 Jan 1985. McPreaz: *Cincinatti Enquirer*, 17 Aug 1901. Balabhai: *Times of India*, 5 Jan 1989. Neagu: *[R]*, 20 July 1991. Omani woman: *[R]*, 19 Feb 1990. Quirino: *D.Express*, 6 April 1989. Castledene: *The People*, 3 Nov 1991. Romanian girl: *[AFP]*, 29 Jan 1992. Allison: *Weekend*, 14 Sept 1997. Lodge: *S.Express*, 8 June 1986. Vorobyeva: *Izevstia*, 14 June 1987. Mdletshe: *[AP]*, 22 March 1993. Mcetywa: *Johannesburg Star*, 24 March 1995. Archer: *Irish Independent, Sun*, 19 March 1996. Garcia: *People and Places (Ghana)*, 17 Oct 1996. Coons: *D.Telegraph*, 14 April 1989. Al-Shaani: *[R]*, 17 Aug 1989, etc.

WHAT DREAMS MAY COME

Thai ghosts: *Independent*, 23 July 1991. Father's voice: *Manatee Herald Tribune*, 18 Feb 1999. Shop-girl: *D.Mirror*, 17 July 1975. Collapsing house: *D.Mirror*, 8 Jan 1974. Dental escape: *S.Post*, 1 June 1975. Slot machine: *St Louis Post-Dispatch*, 3 Sept 1987. Nappy change: *S.Express*, 17 Nov 1985. Escaped mare: *Expressen*, 22 Aug 1995. Collapsing church: *S.Express*, 9 Dec 1984. Elephant dung: *D.Mirror*, 20 Jan 1997. Gas explosion: *S.Express*, 2 April 1972. Bank vault: *D.Express*, 14 Feb 1974. Ulcer: *Sun*, 20 Feb 1986. Sorceress: *Courier Mail*, 10 April 1997. Gas blast: *D.Express*, 3 March 1986.

LAND OF THE LOST

Yeomans: *D.Telegraph*, 23 Oct 1997. Leadbitter: *Guardian*, 23 April 1997. Stanton: *D.Telegraph*, 23 March 1996. Drennen: *Harrisburg Patriot-News*, 5 April 1992. Harris: *[AP]*, 6 March 1991. Ackroyd: *D.Star*, 27 June 1991. Murray: *S.Express*, 3 Feb 1985. Fletoridis: *D.Express*, 24 July 1987. Munden: *Bristol Evening Post*, 10 April 1995. Dixon: *Times*, 2 Nov 1996. Argentine prisoner: *D.Mirror*, 28 Sept 1995. Giese: *Eve. Standard (London)*, 22 Oct 1997. Johnson: *South China Morning Post*, 25 May 1998. Li Qingzhu: *[AP]*, 17 June 1998.

WHAT'S UP, DOC?

Stethoscope: *D.Telegraph*, 9 Oct 1998. Cricket ball: *D.Telegraph*, 1 Aug 1998. Right-hand heart: *[AFP]*, 2 Oct 1997. Stammer: *Sun*, 29 Sept 1997. Hit by train: *[AP]*, 15 Aug 1997. 40 doctors: *D.Telegraph*, 5 May 1998. Deaf-mute: *[AFP]*, 7 Jan 1999. Model plane: *D.Express*, 2 Aug 1977. Broken neck: *D.Star*, 26 May 1994. Self-lobotomy: *Independent*, 26 Jan 1988. Aerial operation: *D.Telegraph*, 15 June 1995.

PLUMMETS

Saggers: *D.Mirror*, 2 April 1993, etc. Lau Tim: *[R]*, 9 Nov 1997. Spanish baby: *[R]*, 27 Nov 1997. Ilie: *Evenimentul Zilei*, 11 March 1998. Burton: *Toronto National Post*, 6 Nov 1998. Wright: *D.Telegraph*, 10 Aug 1988. Lard: *News of the World*, 30 July 1978. Khatoon: *S.Express*, 17 July 1983. Savitska: *D.Telegraph*, 17 Dec 1990, etc. Schwalen: *D.Express*, 26 June 1990. Freemantle: *Western Morning News*, 10 Aug 1993. McClelland: *[AP]*, 5 Sept 1994. Brighton man: *D.Telegraph*, 4 Aug 1990. Israeli man: *The Jewish Week*, 12-18 Feb 1993. Grosjean: *Le Matin (Switzerland)*, 25 July 1995. Smirnova: *[AP]*, 24 May 1997. Palma tourist: *S.Mail*, 19 May 1991. Boyce: *[R]*, 16 April 1992. Hong Kong woman: *S.Express*, 24 June 1990.

ALL AT SEA

Cuban refugees: *NY Post*, ? Aug 1994. Kiribati fishermen (1): *D.Telegraph*, 14 May 1992. Kiribati fishermen (2): *D.Telegraph*, 25 Aug 1986. Filipino fishermen: *[AP]*, 29 Sept 1993. Malaysian fishermen: *D.Telegraph*, 24 Jan 1997. Steen: *D.Telegraph*, 12 July 1991. Hockey: *Sun*, 8 Feb 1995. Korean sailor: *Weekly News*, 23 March 1991. Brighton women: *Times*, 9 Sept 1995. Mayo: *[AFP]*, 1 Dec 1995. Chenery: *D.Telegraph*, 23 Jan 1989. Shiflett: *D.Mirror*, 6 June 1986. Bourse: *D.Mail*, 9 June 1986. Welsh children: *Sussex Evening Argus*, 4 Aug 1992. Barth: *D.Mirror*, 30 Sept 1993. Vandorn: *Middlesbrough Evening Gazette*, 9 April 1997. Hudson River: *D.Mail*, 14 Aug 1986. Chase: *Weekly News*, 15 Oct 1977. Carlsen: *D.Telegraph*, 21 Oct 1992. Balcx: *South China Morning Post* 1 Dec, 1994.

GOLDEN GAMBLES AND RUNS OF LUCK

Turkish lottery: *Hürriyet*, 26 + 28 January 1992. Holes-in-one: *D.Mail*, 9 Feb 1984. Triple survivor: *Aberdeen Evening Express*, 11 Sept 1995. Crowley: *D.Telegraph*, 31 Dec 1993. Run of tails: *Queensland Courier-Mail*, 20 Jan 1995. Betting on 23: *Sun*, 25 Sept 1992. Record roulette repeats: *D.Mail*, 10 Sept 1993. Austrian teacher: *Sun*, 16 Jan 1986. Numbered fish: *Western Morning News*, 16 Sept 1995. Numbered frog: *Guardian*, 25 Jan 1999. TWA 800 bet: *[AP]*, 24 July 1996. Football pools: *D.Record*, 27 Nov 1995. Banks: *Middlesbrough Eve. Gazette*, 25 Nov 1997. Lotterie: *D.Mail*, 17 Dec 1997. Buddhist monk: *Independent*, 25 March 1998. Boa eggs: *Independent*, 28 April 1998. Rock climber: *D.Star*, 24 Nov 1990. Trainspotter: D. Telegraph, 31 July 1984. God's lottery-ticket: *D.Star*, 1 Sept 1981. Frenchman: *Independent*, 15 July 1992. Honeymoon: *Evening Leader*, 22 June 1992. Thoroughgood, *D.Mirror*, 15 June 1991. Shaw: *D.Telegraph*, 22 Dec 1986.

REFERENCES

WEATHER OR NOT

Yang: *D.Telegraph*, 22 June 1985. Waldick: *San Francisco Examiner*, 23 Feb 1998, etc. Hami children: *D.Telegraph*, 30 May 1986. Sam the cat: *D.Mirror*, 25 Aug 1998. Dahran: *Mail on Sunday*, 23 May 1993. Seagrave: *Orange County Register*, 25 Feb 1998. Chidgey: *Canberra Times*, 7 Sept 1997. Mello: *D.Mail*, 12 Aug 1976. Leyden: *D.Mirror*, 28 June 1989.

AND OTHERS...

Seymour: *Independent*, 20 Dec 1991. Martin: *Huntsville Times*, 20 Sept 1985. Moroccan dealer: *Western Morning News*, 5 April 1993. Jones: *Sun*, 3 Aug 1993. Grinston: *[AP]*, 14 May 1995. Button: *D.Mirror*, 26 May 1990. Seal: *D.Mail*, 15 Jan 1996. Crooks: *Wolverhampton Express & Star*, 3 Nov 1995. Armthorpe family: *D.Mirror*, 30 Oct 1991. Gell: *D.Mail*, 9 June 1986. Tramp: *Guardian*, 16 April 1981. Orton: *D.Star*, 9 Feb 1995. Long: *Toronto Sun*, 22 Feb 1981. Pinchin: *D.Mirror*, 5 Dec 1992. Level-crossing: *Guardian*, 28 Nov 1979. Italian hiker: *Times of Malta*, 28 Jan 1998. Tagliabue: *Sun*, 12 April 1994. Trout: *Cleveland Plain Dealer*, 7 March 1991. Mexican train-crash: *Guardian*, 27 Feb 1991. Ewing: *D.Star*, 4 Nov 1989. Singhiana: *Times of Oman*, 1 Sept 1994. Raymond: *South China Morning Post*, 7 Oct 1998. Mombasa lizard: *S.Mail*, 8 Oct 1995. Walters: *Sun*, 15 March 1997. Cooley: *S.Mirror*, 11 Jan 1976. Steuer: *San José Mercury News*, 14 Jan 1989. Dehaes, *D.Mirror*, 21 July 1987. Bogstad: *S.Mirror*, 30 Nov 1980. Mathews: *Western Morning News*, 9 March 1994. Audley, *Weekly News*, 25 Aug 1979. Lee: *D.Mail*, 22 Feb 1995.